UNEXPECTED
TREASURE

UNEXPECTED TREASURE

by **HOPE SAWYER BUYUKMIHCI**

with **HANS FANTEL**

Illustrated by **JOHN PIMLOTT**

Published by
M. EVANS AND COMPANY, INC.,
New York
and distributed
in association with
J. B. LIPPINCOTT COMPANY,
Philadelphia and
New York

This book is dedicated to
W. G. DUNCAN of Kentucky,
whose "bluebird letters"
led me to the treasure.

FOREWORD

ONE day a fifth grade boy was helping me with my
easel after a school chalk talk wherein I had related
simple stories of nature and sketched portraits of animals. Bracing the heavy easel, the boy looked up at me
with shining, wistful eyes, and said, "Are those things
you told us in there really true?"

I assured him they were.

Unexpected really exists. It happened as I've told it.
You may come and see for yourself.

H. S. B.

Oh life—that sweet and precious thing
To man and beast and bird on wing!
To every lowly living thing
Its greatest treasure.

—Janet Graham

ONE

TODAY, as we sit on our porch, my husband Cavit and I look out over two hundred and fifty wild, swampy acres of New Jersey flatland which we turned into a private animal refuge amidst a plague of bulldozers and the blight of urban sprawl.

In building this preserve against all conceivable

odds I became convinced that the true test of man's humanity lies in his attitude toward other creatures. I believe that a man who can learn to respect and to love the ways of many different animals can also get along with his own kind. If we had a culture fostering respect for nature and love of living things, I am sure that we would not suffer the hatreds dividing our own species.

My own involvement with animals began in early childhood. My grandfather, who owned a farm near Watertown in upstate New York, used to take me riding on a haywagon drawn by two heavy horses. To this day I remember the powerful impression of sheer animal strength and beauty made upon me by the rhythmic heaving of their haunches as I watched their slow, majestic gait from the driver's bench. Lurching from side to side, planting their hooves firmly into the soft road, nodding their heads with each step, the two animals were pulling with all their strength.

I watched the muscles trembling as they worked against the load; I saw their breath swell their flanks; and, with the strangely direct perception of a child, I knew that I was in the presence of an enduring mystery.

I cannot pinpoint the earliest moment of my conscious awareness of animals but I must have been still in my pram when it happened. My mother used to supplement our meager family income by baking cakes and carting them to her customers in Watertown in my baby carriage, tucked under the blanket next to me. Her errands, she told me later, were often delayed by my insistence on petting dogs, cats, and delivery horses.

If an interest in nature can be inherited, I might well have come by it from my father's side, for he, a well-known painter of birds, has the keen eye and fine perception of a trained observer. Often we would walk through fields and along the hedgerows, and he would draw pictures for me of everything we saw. I still remember the day—I must have been about six— when he spotted a snake near a stone wall. As we came close, the snake reared up, hissing and playing his forked tongue back and forth. With the back of his neck flared out like that of a cobra, the three-foot-long snake looked formidable, and I was thoroughly frightened. Yet my father calmly reached out and picked him up.

"A puff adder," he said. "See how he's puffed himself up? Take him in your hands. He won't hurt you."

I was afraid. But my father's attitude reassured me. I let the brown-mottled snake glide over my hands and arms, and with a shudder half of revulsion and half of delight, felt the curious coiling motion of the snake's smooth, dry body. I admired his courage when he kept right on rearing, writhing, and hissing, as if he were about to swallow me whole.

"Now put him down," my father said. I laid the snake in the grass. Now my father had another stratagem to show me the snake's odd behavior. "First he tries to bluff you by seeming fierce," he explained.

"But look what he does when he finds out that the bluff doesn't work."

With a stick my father stirred the grass in front of the snake. By planting his boot behind the snake, he prevented his rearward escape. As soon as the snake realized that he was cornered, he stopped his puffing and fierceness. Instead, he tried Plan 2. He turned over on his back, opened his mouth in a pitiful grimace with his forked tongue hanging out grotesquely. He was playing dead in a gruesomely convincing way, looking like the slain dragon in a miniature painting of St. George. Again I picked him up. He remained motionless and I could at leisure inspect his glistening scales, his tiny nostrils, and the graceful delicacy of his face.

I have loved snakes ever since. More importantly, I learned at that time something about the personality of animals—their schemes and devices, their fears, and their cunning in their often desperate struggle to stay alive. Because my father was able to interpret the snake for me, I overcame my initial fear. I learned to respect the snake on his own terms.

Many such lessons were learned in the spring, for, to anyone on a farm, the coming of spring is literally the renewal of life.

The very thought of spring would fill my mind with pictures: the blossom-gleaming apple tree right outside the window; red-winged blackbirds screaming in the branches; the tiny brown peepers trilling in the swamp; and the first robin pulling worms in the yard.

But for me, one event more than any other signaled the return of the warm season. It was the singing of the woodcocks.

In April we once walked down a cowpath bordered with cedars, the earth still damp from late thaws. Packed tight by the ice that not long ago had lain on it, the sun-warmed mud now crumbled beneath my bare feet. We came out in an overgrown field where brush and young poplars made fine bird cover. The air was very quiet.

In the approaching dusk, shadows grew blacker and a chill came into the clear spring air. While the tree tops still caught the red and yellow light of the low sun, the bushes were already mere black outlines billowing against the sky. The sharp contrast between light and shadow was somehow eerie in the stillness of the evening and I began to be afraid.

"Where's the woodcock?" I asked, just to break the silence.

"Sh-h-h," said my father. "Wait."

Suddenly we heard some rustling in the bushes. My father squeezed my hand.

A moment later, with a thudding flurry of his wings, a small bird with a long beak flung himself up into the sky. In steep ascent he gained height until he disappeared from sight—a sign that soon he would begin his haunting song for the female, who was meanwhile waiting in the bushes.

Then out of the clear sky the song reached us. It fell on us from above like a shower—liquid, chortling, and

15

bubbling. An incredible array of exuberant sounds, rising in spiraling trills, and at the last climax stopping abruptly just before the little bird plummeted to the ground. We heard his rasping "Peent!" Peent!" as he stepped his intricate mating dance with patterns as formal as a gavotte.

Several times we saw him rise, swing upward in wide circles, sing his cascading melodies, and then dive back to earth. We watched until the sky grew so dark that we could no longer see him and I was numb with cold. My father carried me home in his arms.

There were many years when my father and I watched the woodcock sing in early April. But I always remember that first time. It was one of the happiest events in my life, and even today, when I hear these lovely, long-beaked birds, I seem to be reliving my childhood.

Another highlight of my childhood farm days was holding a ruffed grouse chick in my hand. My father had been studying the grouse in connection with one of his paintings. As we walked through the woods in spring he showed me several nests and called my attention to the soft booming sound of the male bird beating his wings.

One day we surprised a mother grouse with her brood of two- or three-day-old chicks. The mother flew away, crying. We hid ourselves nearby and my father imitated the beckoning call of a mother grouse. Two of the chicks appeared. He took one outside the woods to photograph, feeding him flies and other insects. Replacing him then where we'd found him, we tried to walk away, but he tumbled after us, peeping frantically, until I took him again in my hand, where he cuddled contentedly; then he climbed to my neck and snuggled under my hair.

At that moment I sensed for the first time the indescribable joy of having made friends with a wild, unbeholden animal. Human association and friendship is always an exchange, a transaction based on some form of mutual interest. The same is true of one's relation to domestic animals. But to make some kind of meaningful contact with a wild animal is to me a matchless thrill. Today, when the beavers on my pond quite casually accept me as their companion, I feel myself greatly honored by their trust.

It took quite an elaborate stratagem to persuade the young grouse to leave us. While I set the chick on the ground, my father imitated the hen's clucking from another direction to lure him away from me. Since he was already busily picking up bugs, we felt quite sure that he would be able to take care of himself when we finally got away from him.

Birds became my main interest at that stage of my life. Their flight, plumage, and song gave me my earliest concept of sheer beauty. With my older brother Laurance, I roamed the rolling hillsides of the farming country near our home, always hoping to observe the many kinds of birds that were still abundant in New York State during my childhood. We avidly searched for nests and tried to identify the various species. In breathless quiet, quivering with excitement, we stalked the birds to observe their habits, and, too poor to own a camera, we made sketches of what we observed.

In all these explorations, we stuck to the rules my father had dinned into us: never disturb a nest; never steal an egg. Father had not presented these rules to us as restrictions. Rather, he made us feel that these are basic points of honor and good manners, and only by observing them would we be fit company for animals.

This made sense to us, even as children. And though Laurance's great passion at the time was collecting bird eggs, he only took eggs from obviously abandoned nests, or infertile eggs that remained in the nest after the young had hatched. I was very pleased that he admitted me as an active partner in the great enterprise of egg-collecting.

Often we would find the egg of a bluebird, robin, or sparrow which had been laid in haste on the ground, far from the bird's nest. Laurance picked up these eggs, pricked them with a pin at each end to blow out their contents; then he placed them in one of his many wooden cigar boxes, which he had compartmented, lined with cotton, and carefully labeled.

Not altogether content with his neat wooden boxes, he wanted to display the eggs in a more natural setting. Since most birds do not use their nests a second time, we found plenty of abandoned nests. We never picked them up right away. We often waited for days to make sure the birds had really left. Then we would take the nests home and create realistic surroundings for them. We made "grass" from green crepe paper, and painted authentic-looking oak and maple leaves which we then stuck to dry twigs arranged around the nests.

Only once did we break our code of never disturbing the living birds, and that time we were unaware of having done it.

I was walking through the cow pasture with Laurance. My hand held a switch made from a mullein stalk. This was a handy weapon with which to decapitate clover and buttercups. Even the tough purple heads of Canada thistle fell mangled before my blows.

As I stepped off the dusty cowpath to fell a thistle, a song sparrow sprang up from the prickly base.

"Laurney! Laurney!" I screeched. "I found a nest."

Laurance leaped down from the wall where he had been jabbing his stick into holes between the rocks. We knelt together and parted the dried grass that grew tangled in the wicked stems of the thistle. The carefully hidden nest lay exposed.

"Man!" he said. "Man!"

The four cream-white eggs thickly speckled with brown were too beautiful just to look at. I put out my hand and laid it gently over them.

"They're still warm," I said.

"Of course. She just left, silly. Don't break them,"

19

Laurance said. "Here, let me feel." His hand was bigger than mine, and I was afraid it might accidentally crush the delicate shells.

The mother bird was crying desperately, sharply, flitting from branch to branch of a hawthorn tree, even daring to light briefly on a mullein stalk a few feet from us to distract our attention. We knew the eggs must not get cold, so we planned to leave right away.

"Wonder when they'll hatch," I said, as Laurance started to lower the grass roof gently back over the next.

"Ought to be any day now," he said. "We'll come every day and check." Then, "Hey!" he exclaimed suddenly. "Look at this egg. It's cracked."

"Then it isn't any good." I suggested.

"Nuts! It must be ready to hatch. I'll bet the bird is trying to get out right now. Let's listen."

The mother bird cried unheeded in the background, as we took turns laying our ears against the egg, trying to catch a signal of life. There was no sound, but as we watched, a tiny chip flaked off one end of the egg and a drop of blood oozed out.

"It's hatching! It's hatching!" We had never seen an egg hatch.

We waited. Nothing more happened. "What's the matter?" I asked.

"I don't know," my brother said.

"Maybe he's stuck," I suggested.

"Yeah, maybe."

In both our minds struggled the same temptation, born of curiosity, of pity—of ignorance. Father had told us that if we ever tampered with an egg it wouldn't hatch. He had even warned us that the baby bird must work hard to escape the shell as a prenatal exercise, or he might die of weakness on the first day of life. But this bird was already hatching. It looked as if he was dying in the attempt. We couldn't leave, and we couldn't stand by without acting.

Laurance did it, but I wanted it done. He widened the crack with his fingertips and picked the shell apart speck by speck with his nail. The naked bird lay squirming feebly in Laurance's palm as we gazed at the traceries of red blood vessels, the circle of his closed eye, and the big, yolk-like bulge of his stomach.

"He's alive," I breathed.

"Yeah. Look at him wiggle."

"Hadn't we better put him back?" I said.

"Yeah."

Laurance gently slid the wet, scrawny baby down into the nest, hurriedly arched the grass over, and we left.

I was proud of what we had done, yet underneath gnawed a feeling of guilt. Maybe Father was right. Perhaps we had harmed the bird. Next morning we went back to the nest. The mother bird flew up again in alarm. The three unhatched eggs were there, along with the baby. But the baby bird was dead.

For all the fascination birds held for us, they were not our only interest. For us, every wild animal was an event. In our woodlot lived dozens of chipmunks, darting among the brush piles and digging their burrows among the roots of pines. We loved to watch these neat, vivacious animals running over the soft beds of old pine needles, their pencil-like tails held upright like the masts of tiny ships.

Laurance and my other brother Joe made many ingenious box traps and managed to catch several chipmunks, putting them in boxes where we planned to keep them as pets. Luckily for them, their sharp teeth and tireless little paws enabled them to dig and scratch their way out every time.

When we weren't in school, or working around the house, Laurance and I spent our days roaming the fields, walking cross-lot for hours. Our parents' friends lived within a radius of ten miles. Each time we went roaming we had the home of one of these friends as our goal. All along the way there were creeks, pastures, and wood patches—the sites of inexhaustible adventure.

In our minds, we made a secret map as we traveled every road and explored every nook of field and forest. At each season we knew where to get the juiciest blackberries, the biggest huckleberries, the sweetest beechnuts. The great chestnut trees that had stood in this region for over a hundred years were dying of blight, but here and there a few healthy trees remained, and we knew where. We kept our knowledge to ourselves, for the nuts were a great prize. Cracking the nuts with stones, we ate our fill. Then we would return to the meadow, fling ourselves on our backs to peer skyward between the giant grass-heads to watch the passage of clouds.

One of our favorite goals was Big Gully, six miles away, a deep, timbered slash in the landscape with a fast-running stream at the bottom where Laurance and I liked to fish. Now and then we caught one. I remember the pang of pity I always felt as the fish flopped on the dry bank, gasping for life. Laurance, too, was touched. But, like so many boys, he thought he owed it to his maleness not to show his feelings. Usually he picked up the fish by the tail, smashing the head against a rock to end the creature's suffering. Sometimes several blows were needed before the fish lay still. I always shuddered at the act of murder. I never liked to see the worm wriggle on the hook or the fish gasping.

I had to get Laurance to bait my hook, though he called me a sissy.

Yet, despite my feelings, I went right on fishing. It was many years before I thought these matters through and made my decision to live as a vegetarian—a resolve which has contributed much to my peace of mind.

Very likely, the crucial childhood experience that in later life made me decide not to live by slaughter was the pig-sticking at a neighbor's farm when I was eight.

It was a cold day in November. Across the road the Joneses had the kettle of hot water ready in the yard for butchering. We got our milk from the Joneses; and every day as I went over with my pail I had seen the pigs rooting in their pen, running up to the bars as I was passing, sniffing, and looking at me with their tiny, eager eyes. I had watched the mother sow lying happily on her side with a dozen pink piglets beside her, grunting contentedly as they nursed. And to me, the little pigs with their charming corkscrew tails and their cozy round shape had been more precious than any doll. Now they were to be cruelly massacred.

"Stop them," I begged my mother.

"There is nothing we can do," my mother said. "The pigs are theirs."

This wasn't a good answer. And even then I knew it. It didn't seem right that a living creature could be property. Instinctively I felt that a living being can never belong to anyone but himself. Now I can formulate this thought. But then I couldn't. I could only watch in horror as the hired man drove the hog toward the steaming kettle, where a gallows had been erected between two great maples.

I screeched: "They're going to kill him!"

"Don't look," said my mother. She went on scrubbing the linoleum. But I couldn't tear my eyes from the window. I saw the heavy club crash down and I heard the pig scream. He wasn't dead, and he was trying to get away. Bending, Mr. Jones slipped a chain around one hind leg and pulled it tight. He and the hired man worked quickly with rope and chain, hauling the heavy animal up high over a bar. The pig was thrashing wildly, screaming in mortal fear. Then Mr.

Jones stepped over and slit his throat. Blood gushed out and there was a choked break in the screaming.

Blind with terror, I stumbled upstairs to my bed, covered my head with my pillow and sobbed. I remained so for hours. My mother tried to comfort me, but I would not even look up at her. I only dug my face deeper into the mattress.

Much later, when I finally let my mother lead me downstairs, I saw a sight that was to haunt me for years. Six hogs under the maples, their gutted bodies propped open with sticks. Their screams still rang in my ears.

The memory of that scene would return later in life whenever I had to witness violence done to animals. One of the most disturbing visions of this kind occurred thousands of miles away after my husband had taken me to his native Turkey.

The year was 1950. Living with my husband's family was a constant round of intercultural skirmishes. If I wanted merely to go sightseeing or shopping, my relatives were shocked at my audacity.

"In America, all women do," explained Cavit, my husband.

This usually produced noisy arguments which I, having a mere smattering of Turkish, could not follow except for the insistent shouts by Cavit's uncle that this was Turkey, not America.

Not until much later did I understand that the restraints they tried to impose on me were, in a way, a form of love. They wanted me to be one of them—to fit into their lives. But it surely didn't help matters that I had grown up as an American farm girl with a tough streak of independence, while they, as one of Turkey's old-line families, tended to be even more tradition minded than most Moslems.

To me it seemed as if I had been transported not just to another country but to another era. My role as a "respectable" woman, I discovered, consisted mainly in sitting at the window all day, awaiting my husband's return. And since Cavit's work as a road engineer for the Turkish government took him away for weeks, it was often a long wait.

I felt the unspoken disapproval of Cavit's grandmother and uncle, with whom we were staying. Clearly, when Cavit had gone to study in America, they had not expected him to bring back such an exotic bride. Even the servants seemed to scorn my outlandish ways. None could understand why I wasn't content to sit at the window, peering out between the curtains that hid my face from outside view.

Beyond these curtains lay Istanbul, Queen of Cities, which I had come halfway round the world to see. Dark men thronged the street, huddled in small groups and haggling with a curious kind of furtive vitality while others sauntered among the jostling traffic with studied leisure.

Everything seemed exotic and mysterious—even a simple load of wood heaped on a cart, for the local timber was all gnarled in a way I had never seen before. Nature itself seemed to underline a strange feeling of twistedness I sensed in my surroundings. Indeed, the domed mosques slicing into the clear sky like fantastic cookie cutters, the tangled arabesques decorating the doorways made me feel that I wasn't living in reality at all, but inhabited a flamboyant stage set. How different it all was from the straight-walled, straight-beamed, wooden houses of my rural American background.

Aching to explore the strange city and the mysterious life of which the view from my window gave but enticing hints, I pointed to the shrouded women I saw scurrying along the walls, implying that perhaps I, too, might be permitted to go out.

"Female servants," Cavit's uncle explained. "Respectable women don't walk in the street."

A visiting relative overheard our conversation. "You," she added slowly, in pidgin Turkish, pointing her sewing needle at me, "married." Now she pointed the needle at her wedding ring. She spoke to me as to a child. Then she slowly elaborated what was expected of me as a wife. "No movies. No tennis. Shameful things. Stay home. Sew." She swept her eyes reproachfully over my skinny frame. "Turkish woman always fat."

She knew of course that women lived and behaved differently in the western world. But since she didn't go to movies and read little, and since television had not yet reached the Near East, her main notion about western women was their supposed wickedness. She had no personal animosity against me. In fact, my hus-

27

band's family was extremely generous, and if I had been able to encourage it, would probably have given me signs of genuine affection. But basically they regarded me as a strange creature to be gradually tamed and civilized.

One facet of my personality, in particular, seemed incomprehensible to my Turkish in-laws—the way I felt about animals. It distressed me to see the often cruel unconcern shown by Turkish draymen to their horses and donkeys. Once, toward the end of our stay, I expressed my feelings in a way that outraged the family.

As usual, I was sitting at the window when I saw a donkey being driven up the hill. He was a scrawny little creature with huge and gentle black eyes. His face bore a look of patient resignation and his round furry flanks were like soft pillows. Piled high on his back was his burden. Chairs, cabinets, strange-looking brass kitchen utensils were arranged in a sort of tower on a platform over the donkey's spine. The awkward pile was clearly top-heavy, and its swaying from side to side made it difficult for the donkey to keep his footing.

Just as he rounded the curve in front of my window, the donkey slipped on a cobblestone. The violent swing of his burden pulled him off his tiny feet, and he came crashing down on his side. The clatter of the household goods scattering on the pavement, mixed with the screaming curses of the driver, created quite a commotion on the street. Rather than unburden the donkey of his load and help him to his feet, the driver began beating him with a strong, knurled stick and twisting his tail. The donkey struggled piteously. Then suddenly, the driver lifted his club, swung it far back, and with a gesture of concentrated malevolence hit the little donkey right in the eye.

I don't know what came over me at that moment. Perhaps it was the memory of a story by Nora Lofts, describing an English woman in India whipping a cruel bullock driver. But I grabbed a heavy cane from the umbrella stand and tried to rush out into the street to rescue the donkey. I don't know what would have happened if I had actually struck the driver. Fortunately, Cavit's uncle restrained me at the door.

Cavit's uncle did not speak to me about it afterward, but I sensed that he and the rest of the family were deeply troubled by the incident. For the sake of a donkey I had risked public disgrace. Obviously, I was totally irresponsible and a threat to the family's reputation. They watched me even more closely from then on. Cavit was away on a field assignment, and I was practically under house arrest.

I sat sullenly at the window for days and weeks. I soon ran out of reading matter, and the family—not wishing to encourage literacy in a woman—pretended not to understand my request for English books.

Thrown entirely on my own resources, I entertained myself with endless ruminations. Sometimes I fancied myself a caged animal. I thought of a small bear I had once seen at a county fair as a child. As it turned out, that thought proved one of the key events in my life, leading me to recognize and revive within myself a feeling of kinship with animals that I have felt ever since early childhood.

It seemed to me that the traditional Moslem attitude toward women was pretty close to man's general attitude toward "other" creatures. Man in the Moslem world considers himself master of woman. He thinks he "owns" her—and, by the laws of the land, he does. Similarly, man everywhere thinks himself the master of other species, and that he owns them by law. But man's laws usually serve his convenience more than they serve justice, and man's mastery is often based on ignorance and is destructive.

I kept pondering these parallels: My in-laws denied me my way of life. Not through malevolence, but through thoughtlessness. What stood between us was a kind of emotional ignorance, a lack of recognition for the needs of the other. Likewise, I felt, man fails to recognize the natural claims of animals.

I enlivened many long hours at my Turkish window with such thoughts, but mostly I dwelled on memories of my childhood. At the time of the equinox, the sun stood in a place where, framed by mosques and minarets, I could see it sink into the dark blue water of the Bosporus—a sight of breathtaking, exotic beauty. But to me, in my homesickness, it only recalled the sunsets at the farm when my eyes followed the red sun down, watching it brush the treetops and then slowly creeping behind them. It was right there in the woods! I asked my brother Laurance if we could run over there and touch it. He said no. But I kept wondering why.

It was at my window in Turkey that I was reminded with the most excruciating vividness of the slaughter of the Joneses' pigs. It was during the feast of *Kurban Bayram*, the Feast of Sacrifice.

"Look at all the sheep!" I exclaimed to Cavit. Our street was crowded with a flock of sheep and lambs, being driven along by a tattered herdsman calling "*Koyun! Koyun!*"

"What's up?" I asked.

"They're for *Kurban*," Cavit said, trying to sound offhand. He gave me an odd look, and then suddenly remembered that he had to go to his room to look for something.

Just then our neighbor Mehmet came out on his balcony and called down to the shepherd, who halted his flock. The sheep immediately began to graze on wisps of grass and weeds along the wall. Each rump was decorated by a bright patch of red color. Mehmet Bey came down, and bargaining began.

"Fifty lira," the sheepman said.

"No!" said Mehmet, tipping his head back and clicking his tongue against the roof of his mouth in the Turkish negative. "Not more than twenty-five."

"Impossible."

Mehmet was shrewd. "See how scrawny they are!" he said.

"No! No! Fat," the seller said. "Look at their tails." Each of the sheep had a doughnut of fat around his tail. They were of the breed called fat-tails, and the fat rendered from their tails was much prized as shortening.

"No, no," Mehmet said impatiently. "They are not what I want." He turned to go back in the house.

The owner of the sheep followed, touching his arm. "All right," he said, "I'll make it forty-five lira—for you."

Mehmet's head went back in scorn, and his tongue clicked. He strode toward the steps. The herder ran in front of him, gesticulating and jabbering. Mehmet stopped with his foot on the first step. "Thirty, then," he said. "That's my last offer."

"I can't do it. I'd lose money," wailed the man, but he leaned on the rail in such a way that Mehmet could not pass. "You can have it for thirty-five," he said. "Let me make something, to live."

Brushing aside the man's arm, Mehmet continued up the steps and started into his house. Just as the door was about to close, the sheepherder yelled, "Wait! Take it for thirty." As the money changed hands both men smiled broadly, pleased with their bargain.

Mehmet looked the sheep over carefully and pointed to a white lamb with an exceptionally fat tail. Fishing a string from his waistband, the herder tied it around the neck of the lamb, and handing the end to Mehmet, rounded up the others and strolled on, calling, *"Koyun! Koyun!"*

The white lamb followed meekly as Mehmet led him to the side yard and tethered him to a stake.

Down the street, the sheepherder stopped again to haggle with other neighbors. I saw Bayan Lutfi pick out a plump, brown sheep and tie him to her gate. By that time, Cavit had returned, realizing that he could no longer evade my questions.

"Next week is *Kurban Bayram*," he said. "All those who can afford it buy a sheep or lamb for sacrifice."

"You mean they kill them."

"Yes. That's what they buy them for."

"How do they do it?"

"You'll see," Cavit said uncomfortably. "I have to go to work now."

Sometimes he was at a loss to explain native customs to me, and he knew that the idea of ritual slaughter was profoundly upsetting to me. Willfully to destroy a living creature—God's noblest work—for religious reasons seemed to me the most revolting sacrilege.

The children in the street were happily romping about with the sheep and lambs, petting and coddling them. Later, the same children watched transfixed with fascination, as the bleating lambs were held by their hind legs and the men, carrying long knives, advanced on their helpless victims.

What kind of people would these children become if love and murder were so early interlinked in their minds?

Before dinnertime, Mehmet's wife, Elif Hanim,

came to the door with a pan full of raw lamb. "Happy holiday," she said, her face lit with generosity and the joy of the feast.

"Thank you," I said, accepting the gift.

TWO

CHILDREN are naturally passionate. They have an innate capacity for being entranced. Their kind of childish rapture is closely akin to the sense of wonder that, in adult life, marks the artist and the creative scientist. It is sad that this marvelous freshness and intensity of childish feeling and perception so rarely survives our deadening educational progress or the many disillusionments which we lump together under the name of "growing up."

My own passion as a child was drawing. To create on paper, with colored crayons, my own vision of reality was for me a profoundly mysterious and totally absorbing activity.

I may have come by this bent toward the graphic arts through imitating my father, who not only was a professional artist but often drew pictures illustrating the stories he told to us.

My family was too poor to provide me with sketch pads, but I soon discovered that the fifty-pound flour bags, which were part of the family's supply of groceries, could be cut up after use to yield yard upon yard of wonderful tough paper on which I would endlessly draw animals and trees.

I sensed that these drawings were quite crude, and my father suggested that I might improve my technique by tracing the work of more accomplished artists. I begged my mother to soak wrapping paper in kerosene to make it semi-transparent. I filled acres of this homemade tracing paper with birds and animals copied from the nature books in my father's library.

One picture in particular I drew over and over again—a male bluebird sitting among pink apple blossoms with a pale blue sky around him. The original bluebird survived more kerosene-soaked overlays than any other picture in the house. As it turned out, it was this picture, probably above any other factor, that determined the course of my life. It led to my training as an artist, which in turn led to meeting my exotic husband. And for both of us, the persistent image of that bluebird helped to define a goal and a vision—the creation of our wildlife preserve.

I was still in grade school when the bluebird for the first time gave a decisive turn to my life. At that time, I was uncommonly shy. I was, in fact, almost paralyzed by shyness. I never spoke to the other children. It was even an enormous effort for me to raise my eyes and look anyone in the face. But my teacher, Miss McGivney, was a person of rare kindness and understanding. Although I never showed my drawings to anyone, she had seen the outline tracings I brought with me to school in order to fill in the colors during my spare moments. Among these pictures she must have noted the recurrent bluebird.

One day during a classroom lesson on native birds, Miss McGivney spoke of the bluebird as one of the earliest to come back each spring. As the herald of spring, she said, the bluebird has become the symbol of hope and happiness.

Her words struck a warmly responsive note in my mind, but I was terrified when next I heard her call my name: "Would you come to the blackboard please and draw a picture of the bluebird for us? What colors will you need?" She held out a box of chalk.

Somehow my legs took me to the front of the classroom. Trembling, my fingers picked out the red, blue, green, and brown chalks. Then I suddenly forgot about Miss McGivney and my schoolmates. The picture I had traced so often took hold of me and guided my hand on the blackboard. Lost in the sheer delight of the colored chalks I put the picture on the board. Then I stumbled back to my seat, head down, overwhelmed with embarrassment—and joy. Dimly I heard Miss McGivney praising my picture. Her praise was the first crack in the cage of my shyness.

Under the sympathetic guidance of Miss McGivney I practiced drawing by endlessly copying the pictures I found in old school books. Many of them so fascinated me that I did them over and over again—like a musician repeating a favorite song. One was a woodsman seated before a campfire, with smoke curling against midnight trees and a small white moon peering through. It was all done in shades of nocturnal blue except for the fire glittering on the camper's face. Another was a wooded lake at sunset. But my favorite during my early school years, copied from the *National Geographic,* showed a wild horse standing in snow with the wind whipping about him, riffling his shaggy mane. I still remember how hard it was to capture the bleak expression on the horse's face.

Copying such pictures may not have prepared me to appreciate contemporary art styles, but it gave me a certain assurance and proficiency in basic drawing skills. With my father's encouragement and instruction, I developed my draftsmanship to the point where I could later work as a professional illustrator to help with college expenses. I couldn't have asked for a more congenial assignment. I was to provide drawings for *The Fieldbook of Natural History* by Dr. E. Laurence Palmer, a member of the faculty at Cornell.

But the pay was low, and to supplement my meager supply of money I took a part-time job slinging hash at the Eddygate Restaurant, just off campus at the top of the hill.

One night at the Eddygate I had some troublesome customers—four swarthy young fellows, jabbering incomprehensibly in a language I had never heard. Obviously, they were having trouble with the menu.

"What it?" one of them asked, pointing to "ANY JUICE 10¢." I made the motion of raising a glass.

"Ah! Drinkings!" he said. He smiled at me, his green eyes crinkling. "Where food?"

I pointed to the entrees. Three of my customers began busily flipping through their pocket dictionaries. But the green-eyed one jumped up. "Kitchen!" he said.

"Chicken, you mean?" I suggested.

"No," he shouted. "KITCHEN!!"

He suddenly grabbed my hand. "Come!"

He jerked his head toward the kitchen. "Go!" Before I could wring myself from his grip, we charged straight into the kitchen through the wrong half of the swinging door, narrowly missing a waitress on her way to the dining room with a tray full of dishes.

He pulled me to the stove, lifting the cover from each steaming pot, peering and sniffing. Spaghetti sauce and chicken a la king left him unmoved, but when he came upon the fragrantly simmering beef stew, his face lit up. "Good," he said. His eye fell upon a big bowl full of tossed salad and his hand shot out. "Good," he said, pointing imperiously, and led the way back to his table.

The four dark men went into a huddle as the green-eyed one reported his findings. Finally agreement was reached, and he was ready to give his order. "Good. Many," he said. I understood and wrote out a ticket for four beef stews with tossed salad. My customers ate their stew with obvious appreciation, and as they left, they said, "Thank you," effusively. When I cleared the table, I found under each plate a fifty-cent tip—an overwhelming generosity in those days.

The four men kept coming back to the Eddygate nearly every night, always insisting on a table in my section of the restaurant. Communication between us was rather halting at first, but a crash program in English at the college soon improved their fluency. Eventually I learned that they were from Turkey, sent by their government to study engineering in the United States. I soon began to look forward to their nightly appearance at the restaurant, and the manager didn't mind if I spent a good deal of time talking with them—particularly the green-eyed one. After all, they were regulars, and they were *my* customers.

A few weeks later, on a Sunday afternoon, I met the green-eyed one right outside my rooming house. "Kismet!" he said, his face beaming.

I wasn't at all sure that this meeting was pure hap-

40

penstance, but to this day I don't know how he found out where I lived. For the first time in our acquaintance he introduced himself formally. His name was Cavit. Soon we were inseparable, going to movies, dances, and other campus events. As soon as I discovered that Cavit, like me, had a profound feeling for nature, I began taking him to my favorite places in the beautiful surroundings of Ithaca. In early springtime we went out in the chilly mornings to see flocks of migrating birds come through the dawn. We watched companies of robins flitting through the bare trees or combing the ground for worms, now and then taking a sip of water which flowed from melting snow in bright rills to join the brook. I particularly remember, some weeks later, walking hand in hand with Cavit through a blossoming apple orchard where the trees, still wet after rain, had a haunting fragrance. Down Fall Creek and Cascadilla Gorge we wandered, and sometimes we would hear the warble of a bluebird, and we would crane our necks to find him in the foliage, but with the tumbling brook in our ears it was hard to spot a bird.

By that time, Cavit's English had progressed remarkably, and we were able to engage in those murky discourses on the meaning of life by which young people indirectly advise each other that—perhaps without realizing it—they have fallen in love.

We favored a rustic stone parapet jutting from a footbridge over Fall Creek; and with the water cascading beneath our feet, and wood thrushes calling

41

from the deep shade, we expounded to each other on the disparate worlds of an American farm girl and a young Turkish gentleman.

Those conversations already established the pattern of our lifelong relationship—the bridging of vast differences through affection and the willingness to admit alternative viewpoints. Like most Americans, I had not been accustomed to values and attitudes other than those supported by local tradition. Learning to see the world through the eyes of an upper-class Moslem was to me an adventure. And to Cavit, who was brought up in the authoritarian traditions of a rigidly stratified society, my American notions of democratic permissiveness were equally new intellectual territory.

Religion was not much of an issue between us. My Christianity could be summed up in the Golden Rule, and its basic notion of fair play is by no means alien to the Koran. Decency and charity seemed to us the central themes of both our faiths, and it seemed incomprehensible to Cavit and me that for centuries Moslems and Christians have been brutally slaughtering each other for the sake of such lovely ideas.

Whatever differences existed between Cavit and me were somehow bridged by our common interest in nature. Many of the animals and trees we saw in our wanderings around Ithaca were strange to him, but he was always eager to learn about them. Sitting under a tree near Beebe Lake one evening, we saw a large skunk majestically ambling toward us. He was a member of one of several skunk families living on campus, and I had already met some of them while strolling in the dusk just before nightfall. This one was a particularly handsome individual, jet black with a broad, brilliantly white stripe down his back, and a tail held proudly erect. He waddled about in the pompous manner of full-grown skunks, swaying from side to side with each step, yet maintaining an aura of serene dignity.

Cavit jumped up. *"Kedi! Kedi!"* he called, and leaning down toward the ground he went toward the little animal with a beckoning hand.

"Wait!" I yelled. "It's not a kitty!"

He was getting closer to the skunk, in his impulsive way apparently bent on stroking the thickly bristling fur.

The skunk stopped and swung his rear toward Cavit, waiting. The azimuth was right. Now the little creature waited for Cavit to come within range of his peculiar artillery.

I jumped toward Cavit in what must have been the nearest thing to a flying tackle. Grabbing his sleeve, I pulled him away, averting the skunk's imminent barrage at the last moment.

Breathlessly I explained the facts about skunks, thinking that Cavit would be eternally grateful to me for his rescue. But he merely shrugged his shoulders: "American-type cat, I thought."

In return for such instruction, Cavit told me of animals and landscape of his country. He had a gift for storytelling; and his hit-or-miss approach to the English vocabulary merely increased the vividness of his descriptions. He recounted for me his journeys by donkey through the mountains of Asia Minor, and conjured up visions of walled gardens haunted by spiky hedgehogs and high-domed land turtles, replete with apricot and almond trees, where nightingales sang beneath the moon. I drank in his stories. *The Arabian Nights* had come alive for me through Cavit.

Yet for all our shared feelings about nature, Cavit's attitude was quite different from mine. He was content to be an observer, basically indifferent. I, by contrast, saw nature as a responsibility. Everywhere man was intruding upon and destroying the animal world. I felt that I had to preserve and protect endangered creatures.

Cavit's attitude, shaped by centuries of Eastern stoicism and resignation, was different. He felt that all things in this world must take their own course and that no man could alter it. He never interfered. Our first quarrel was about that—and many others followed.

Yet one incident during that summer of our courtship convinced me that Cavit would ultimately be capable of shaking off the traditional stoicism of the Turks and allow his natural compassion to come to the fore.

We were exploring an unfamiliar gorge one afternoon. Cavit led the way, holding my hand with one of his while he grabbed at bushes with the other, swinging us both along the steep incline of the gorge. As we scrambled over sliding rocks, our feet sent gray showers of stone leaping down to sink with a flurry of bubbles into the deep water below. I was afraid, but Cavit was laughingly confident.

Suddenly I heard a faint cry above the rush of the water. Cavit had heard it, too. "Listen!" he said, holding me back.

There it came again, from high up across the gorge. It sounded like a child crying. Cavit's face set into a curious cast I had never seen on him before—not so much an expression of determination but rather of a kind of stern inevitability. Silently, he pulled me ahead until we were directly across the gorge from the sound source. It was almost a sheer drop down to the river. Cavit dug his feet into some loose shale and gripped a bush for support. I crawled, relying on my knees to keep me from slipping.

The crying came again. This time we saw its source. A small white puppy was trying to get up the opposite bank, scrabbling for a foothold, which he gained momentarily, then lost again as all four feet slipped on the crumbly rock. As the puppy felt himself slide, he yelped pitifully. Then, suddenly, he was caught and held by a clump of weeds which suspended him above the raging current.

It seemed that there was little we could do. We ourselves were in much the same predicament, and I didn't see how we could get out. The way ahead lay even steeper and the bushes giving us support were

45

thinning. Above us was an overhang. We couldn't climb up.

"You stay here," Cavit said. "I go."

"Where?" I gasped.

He gestured to the other side of the chasm where the little dog lay panting, sprawled against the frail weed. Before I could shout "No!" Cavit had let go of the bush he was holding. Now he was slipping and flailing down the bank, right toward the rapids beneath us. I was horrified, but I couldn't look away. In dreadful anticipation I saw him swept away in the current, but just before he reached the water's edge, he broke his fall by whirling his body about to grab a broken-off tree stub. A moment later, his feet struck a firm rock ledge just at the water's rim. Later he told me that he had noticed that ledge before when some rock pieces we had loosened bounced off it into the water. The ledge wasn't much but enough for him to take a chance.

I watched in continued horror as Cavit crossed the rapids in a series of wide jumps that carried him precariously from stone to stone in the rock-strewn river. Between these treacherous footings, the current ran deep and swift. But at last he gained the other side, and, pulling himself up by grasping at scraggly bushes, he finally reached the whimpering puppy.

I was too exhausted for joy. Helplessly I clung to my place. "Go back to the bridge!" Cavit shouted from across the chasm. I crawled and side-slipped all the way to the bridge, where Cavit was already waiting. Wordlessly he handed me the puppy.

Somehow I sensed that this marked our engagement. The man whose entire background had taught him never to interfere with fate had risked his life for the sake of a puppy. I knew he had done it for me as much as for the dog.

My family wasn't pleased by the news that I was going to marry a Turk, any more than Cavit's family was pleased by his marrying an American. One of Cavit's brothers, I am told, promptly announced that he was going to kill me. My mother, a devout Seventh-Day Adventist, sincerely believed that I would suffer damnation for marrying a heathen, and she prayed for me desperately. My infernal prospects did not lessen her affection for me, and she remained friendly and emotionally close. But that only deepened her sorrow at the thought of my being damned. My father, by contrast, took the matter rather quietly, merely saying he was glad that I was marrying a man I truly liked.

An aunt of mine, judging the matter by her own lights, wrote me that I shouldn't marry Cavit because Sawyer was a good American name whereas Buyukmihci, Cavit's family name, definitely wasn't. I wanted to reply that Buyukmihci was a good Turkish name. But then I thought of something more to the point. "All names," I wrote her, "are good American names."

It was a year later, on a cold, misty day in February

of 1949, that Cavit and I bundled up Nedim, our baby
boy, along with a few other belongings to set off for
Turkey. Cavit had completed his engineering studies,
and had been ordered to return in order to meet his
obligation to work for his government. As far as the
Republic of Turkey was concerned, I was something
of a surprise package. It was strictly against the rules
for Turkish students abroad to get entangled with for-
eigners, let alone marry one of them. By confronting
his high-placed superiors with my undeniable existence—with little Nedim for added emphasis—Cavit, in
a minor way, had scored a *coup d'etat*.

Of our long sea voyage aboard a small Turkish
freighter I mainly remember one incident that was
tragic for me. Characteristically, it had to do with animals. Like many small vessels, our ship had a galley
cat. Her name was "Mestan," and the sailors made
much fuss over her, saying that she was the only Turkish female aboard. The fat captain would repeatedly
tell of Mestan's adventures. The American health
authorities had forced the captain to post a five-
hundred-dollar bond to ensure that Mestan would not
come ashore. "She did go ashore, though," he shouted.
"And brought back a souvenir, like all sailors." The
rest was roared out with vast guffaws and appropriate
gestures. I gathered that Mestan was due to have kittens.

For several days, flocks of gulls accompanied us,
soaring serenely over the ship, never seeming to tire in
hundreds of miles of flight. They were my escort from

48

home—from America—and they gave me a queer ache. Gradually, as we approached mid-Atlantic, the gulls deserted us.

But we encountered other birds, whose flight had been less circumspect and who seemed to have over-shot their range. In mid-ocean, two small grey birds landed on the ship's rail, fluffing their feathers and twittering. Word of their arrival quickly spread among the sailors, and many came to look at them. Nobody had seen their kind before and none could identify them. Evidently they were lost—far off their accus-tomed flightways.

Zeki, the cabin boy, managed to catch one by fling-ing his coat over the rail. He kissed and petted the exhausted little creature, crooning endearing words. Another sailor darted to his cabin and brought a small dish of fresh water and some crumbs which he set on the deck. Zeki released the bird, who flutterd dazedly to the floor and eagerly pecked at the crumbs.

Suddenly, a dark shape dropped through the air. Mestan, jumping from the captain's bridge, pounced upon the hapless bird. The act of murder was too swift for anyone to interfere with it. Later, Zeki, with tears in his eyes, threw the limp tuft of feathers overboard. The other bird, who had watched from the railing, uttered the forlorn cry by which so many birds bemoan the loss of a mate. Then he slowly flew off into the endless sky.

Somehow the death of the little bird profoundly unsettled me. Throughout the voyage I had anxious forebodings about the strange land for which I was heading. Yet my first view of the Turkish shore, from the harbor of Iskenderun, overwhelmed me with its beauty. Rimmed by a crescent of beach, the city clustered next to the ink-blue sea. Shore winds played with the airy fronds of palms along the coast while snowcapped mountains towered beyond.

For the first few days in Turkey, I was entranced with the kaleidoscope of new impressions: oranges, calendulas, pansies, and roses along the streets; ragged children everywhere, their wooden shoes worn to slivers; high-wheeled cabs drawn by skinny horses, their brass-trimmed harness festooned with blue beads; cobbled streets with tumbledown stone houses; men and donkeys sharing the street on equal terms.

But, as a woman brought up in a western culture, I soon came to despise Turkish customs and attitudes. The sight of women walking a respectful distance behind their husbands somehow enraged me, as did the separate entrance for women on streetcars and buses. I would bristle whenever one of my in-laws reminded me that, according to a local proverb, "Heaven is under your husband's foot." In Turkey I came to feel that sexual segregation had but one purpose—to signify that women are a "lower" species—some kind of livestock unfit for the company of men except in the harem.

It bothered me to see Turkish men idly sitting, smoking and drinking in the cafes and along the sidewalk all day, smugly enjoying their leisurely gossip, while their women were locked away at home, laboring to maintain their households in the face of such male indolence.

It also oppressed me that many Turks seemed oblivious to the beauty of their land. When I admired their mountains, they replied: "Wait until you see the new skyscrapers in Ankara." When I spoke of the lovely little donkeys in the streets, they said: "But now we are getting more diesel trucks." They seemed obsessed with the idea of mechanical progress and contemptuous of natural beauty and all the lovely and charming aspects of their ancient country. I certainly have no quarrel with economic advancement, but I cannot help wondering why it so often leads to false values through which nature is degraded and despoiled and machines are exalted beyond living things.

Living with Cavit's family made it quite clear that I could never accustom myself to the ways of my husband's country. Cavit, too, had tasted too much of the heady American mixture of self-determination and personal independence ever to fit comfortably into the tight structure of Turkish bureaucracy. But he loved his country and his family. For him, too, it was a time of conflict and questioning.

As I look back at it now, I can see that my experience in Turkey was really no different from that of many foreign-born people in America. I know a Swiss girl in New Jersey whose marriage to an American was wrecked by family pressure to "Americanize" her. Luckily, my own instincts of self-preservation, and my love for Cavit, proved stronger than the shock of being transplanted to an alien world. On the contrary, in the long run, the experience of confronting each other's contrasting backgrounds in such a direct, intense fashion has created between Cavit and me a kind of bond that would be harder to achieve in a more conventional marriage.

It was during this period of searching for some anchor of meaning amidst the crosscurrents that threatened to swamp our marriage that the idea of the wildlife refuge took shape in my mind. At first, it was merely a vague notion of wanting to live in the country, surrounded by animals and close to the sustaining realities of nature. Out west, I thought, in Washington perhaps, where Cavit and I had spent our honeymoon on an abandoned farm, high on the slopes of Mount Baker.

If we couldn't afford a farm, at least we might have just a piece of land with streams and woods sufficient to give some shelter to forest animals, and, along the forest edge, enough open land for bluebirds to enjoy. Could I make Cavit see it?

I said nothing to him at the time, for he was bitterly struggling with himself. His loyalty was to country; his love was for me; and his wish was to live in America. He spoke little of this, but I felt his turmoil. At times, as if to make up for his "disloyal" thought of leaving Turkey, he became more vociferously Turkish than ever. He would neglect me and speak harshly to me, as if indirectly to remind me what a Turk expects of his wife. At other times, the pendulum of his inner indecision swung in the other direction, and he and I felt a wonderful sense of loving solidarity.

What finally helped resolve these conflicts was the little donkey I tried to rescue when he was so cruelly beaten in front of our house. When Cavit returned after a long field trip, his uncle practically greeted him at the door with an account of my misdeed.

"For a donkey!" the uncle shouted. "She'd shame the family for a donkey!"

Cavit said nothing in my defense. Nor did he reproach me. He understood his uncle's feelings. And he understood mine.

He ate in silence and spent the evening reading quietly. Later, after we had gone to our room, he announced his decision to return to America.

THREE

MY heart leapt at the thought of returning home. In my imagination I pictured us on a farm in the western mountains, perhaps near Mount Baker, where Cavit and I had spent such a happy time before. I envisioned clear brooks sparkling in their rocky beds and looked forward to seeing bears ambling down into the orchards during winter to munch on windfalls.

Whatever the future might hold, there was no doubt in my mind that animals would play an important role in our lives. After the incident with the donkey, I began to regard my feelings about animals in a new light. My impulsive attempt to rush out into the street to rescue the beaten donkey revealed to me that my feeling about animals was something far deeper than liking: it was love, willing to take risks and responsibility.

To be happy, I realized, I had to find a way to give meaningful expression to this love. The thought of creating an animal refuge returned and took hold of me. I wanted to buy land and present it to the animals as a gift. After all, so many creatures had lost their natural habitat as man pushed back the wilderness. In a small way, I wanted to repay their loss.

When I at last broached this to Cavit, he made it quite clear that an animal sanctuary wasn't his idea of a good real estate investment. "You're crazy," he grumbled. "Animals don't pay rent."

I couldn't argue with that. I had been poor enough to know the value of money. But I also knew deep within me that all living things, in a way, belonged to my own family. To spend money for them wasn't squandering it. Someday, I felt, Cavit would see that. But first we had to get out of the country.

The Turkish government had no intention of letting Cavit go back to America. They had paid for his education abroad; now they felt entitled to keep him in service at home. It took every kind of subterfuge to get our exit visa. Even when we were already aboard ship, we still felt that government officials might come chasing after us to haul us back. And under the strict Turkish monetary regulations, we were allowed only about a hundred dollars to take with us.

We reached New York at last on a bright day in the spring of 1954. Two little girls, Linda and Nermin, had meanwhile been added to our family. As we all stood on deck looking at the Statue of Liberty, I felt like an immigrant in my own country.

At the dock we tallied up our assets.

Expenses during the long trip had eaten into our last reserves but I hadn't realized how close we were to destitution.

"You count it," I said to Cavit, hoping he'd somehow come up with a bigger sum.

"Seventy-three dollars and thirty-five cents," said Cavit.

In the brief silence that followed, the dream of Mount Baker collapsed. Setting out across a continent with three children and less than a hundred dollars seemed foolhardy. We were stranded, and on the evening of our return to my homeland we found ourselves dependent on the hospitality of friends in Philadelphia. On the train from New York, we passed through the dismal industrial region of northern New Jersey. Junkyards alternated with ramshackle houses and smoke-belching factories.

"When do we get to America?" asked Nedim, who was old enough to sense that these surroundings were not what we had pictured as our destination. I didn't have the courage to tell him that this, too, was America.

"Soon," I said. "We'll get there soon."

A few days later—down to nearly our last dollar—we telephoned a friend whom we had known at Cornell and who shared our love of nature.

"I've got a trailer," he said. "It's parked in the woods in southern New Jersey. I go there to camp out on weekends. You can live in it till you find something better."

So, instead of becoming western mountaineers, we wound up as swamp-dwellers in the Jersey flatlands.

The low-lying land, laced with still waters, was far different from the snow-peaked mountains for which we had hoped, but I soon became attuned to the endless dialogue between the sky and the marshes as they reflected each other's moods at various times of the day.

Cavit found an opportunity to practice his specialty of metallurgical engineering at a laboratory within commuting distance, and by fall his salary enabled us to move out of our friend's trailer and make the down payment on a house with three acres of land.

As winter faded, I looked over the snowbanks for bluebirds—those childhood companions I had missed so much during my years in Turkey. I listened for the small sounds of their warbling amidst the gusts of the March wind. But none came.

I soon learned why. I chanced upon an article by

Robert Gannon in *Audubon Magazine* describing the plight of the bluebird, driven to near extinction in the short span of a few years by a combination of urban sprawl and the indiscriminate use of insecticides. The article also alerted me to the work of a handful of men dedicated to the preservation of the bluebird, notably Dr. T. E. Musselman of Illinois, who successfully restored bluebirds to his state by putting up hundreds of bluebird houses in relatively protected locations. I learned of W.G. Duncan of Louisville, Kentucky, who brought back the bluebird to regions where it had already become a rare sight, and I began reading Mr. Duncan's "Bluebird Letters," which cover the whole range of wildlife conservation. I came to feel that, if I succeeded in bringing bluebirds back to southern New Jersey, I would have done my small part in restoring the marvellous web of life which mankind has so disastrously torn.

Of the many wonderful pages of Mr. Duncan's, one passage in particular struck me:

Bring back the bluebird! My interest in bluebirds goes back to my early childhood. It was then I first became fascinated by the study of bluebirds, robins, doves, bob-whites, rabbits, ground hogs and a myriad of other forms of wildlife. They flourished at that time along the roadsides, rail fences and all the beautiful, brush-grown fence-rows of rural Kentucky, where I lived. That was long before the State Highway Department moved in with its brown and poisonous sprays, weedkillers and tree destroyers—along with the utility companies and the railroads.

There were many factors involved in the study of these beautiful bluebirds that I found appealing. First they did not build their nests in the blackberry briars and hawthorn, like the catbirds and mockingbirds. Instead, the bluebirds hunted out cavities and empty woodpecker holes in ancient apple trees and hollow fence posts. In these cavities the bluebird built a nest of yellow grass and in this chalice I often found four or five blue eggs. Occasionally the eggs were white.

When sunsets lose their beauty, and the joyful burst of a mockingbird's song no longer enthralls the heart, only then will I forget that first bright April morning, when suddenly a smallish bird, with bright blue feathers, exploded from a hole in a hollow wood fence post, on the sunny hillside of a Kentucky farm. The century and I were young. The heart of a barefoot boy in blue jeans was delighted, with a happiness that has come down through the intervening years. Roger Peterson and John Kieran have pointed out that in most persons a deep love of birds nearly always starts with some special bird that sets off a chain reaction very early in life.

Following the example of Stiles Thomas in northern New Jersey, I built a number of bluebird houses and set them out on our land, hoping to provide the bluebirds with nesting facilities of which the growing cultivation of the countryside had deprived them. But the longed-for bluebirds didn't come, and commoner species, mostly starlings and sparrows, took over the houses I had built.

Another spring came and went. We had been back two years and still no bluebirds had visited us. My nostalgic longing for them grew. I began talking about them to my son. "Have you ever seen a bluebird?" I asked.

"Yes, lots of them," said Nedim. "Don't you remember how they nested over in the maple tree?"

"I don't mean 'blue jay,'" I said. "Bluebird. Do you know what a bluebird is?"

"Do they live around here?" asked Nedim.

"They should," I said. With a pang I realized that my children had missed one of nature's greatest delights. If I couldn't show them a living bird, at least I could tell them about it. So I dug out the pamphlets and brochures I had collected about bluebirds, and together we began reading. Once again I reviewed the reasons for their scarcity: bluebirds live in orchards and gardens—the very places where the mindless spraying of DDT wreaks genocide among many species. And then, unexpectedly, I came upon a hint as to why our own bluebird shelters had not attracted their intended tenants. I had previously overlooked a remark in one of the booklets that bluebird houses should not be placed close to human habitations.

On our three acres, it seemed, we just couldn't get the birdhouses far enough from the dooryard. This doesn't bother sparrows. But bluebirds like to be a bit farther away from people.

Bluebirds came up for a rather heated discussion between Cavit and me one afternoon when we were helping our neighbor, Joe Maurer, hoe corn on his farm. Joe hadn't seen any bluebirds on his land either. I pointed out the probable reason. He had cut off his trees as fast as they reached pulpwood size. No dead stumps were left standing. In all his hundreds of cultivated acres, there were few hedgerows and no rotten posts where a bluebird could find shelter.

"When I lived on a farm," I later said to Cavit, "the woods used to have dead stumps and hollow trees all over. And some would be along the edge of the forest, where the bluebirds like to live. But nowadays the farmers trim out everything."

Cavit nodded, wondering what I was getting at. His hoe clattered amidst the young corn.

So I came right out with it. "What we need," I declared, "is the right kind of land for putting up bluebird houses. We should have a creek or a pond with lots of rotten stumps. And it has to be big enough. How does ten acres strike you?"

"It strikes me right between the eyes," Cavit said firmly. "I'm still paying the mortgage on our place and we've got to save for the kids' education."

He aimed a vicious blow at the next weed. Then he stopped to wipe away the sweat from his forehead. That was all we said then, but I could tell by the look in his eyes that the topic was not closed.

In fact, it was Cavit who brought it up again. Without preamble, and from behind his newspaper, he suddenly said about a week later: "Anyhow, we can ask how much land sells for around here"

Traveling to town the next day, I studied every place that was for sale. A few were tracts with small ponds or bordering small streams. Jotting down the names of realtors, I came home jubilant, and dashed to the phone to dial the first number on my list.

"That eight-acre place on Main Road," I said. "How much do you want for it?"

"Let's see. Is that the one with the pond on the south side?"

"Yes, that's it."

"Let me look. Ah-h-h, let's see.. . ."

My ear was glued to the phone.

"A beautiful place," the realtor assured me. "Perfect for a trailer camp or a group of summer cottages. Five hundred feet of frontage, you know. We priced it low at eight thousand dollars."

"Thank you," I said. "Don't you have anything else, cheaper? Maybe on a dirt road, or back in the woods?"

"Yes," he said smoothly. "Here's a five-acre wooded tract. Back on a township road, but as it builds up there, the road will be improved. There's a small house on the place, too. Only six thousand dollars."

"Is there water on it?"

"No, but you're not far from a lake where there's public swimming and fishing."

"We want land that's not good for anything else," I kept on, though stricken. "We want to preserve wildlife."

"Wildlife? Here's just the thing. I have a nice little farm of twenty acres, with a fair house on it. It's right next to the State Hunting and Fishing Grounds. Just the thing you want, and it's a bargain. The house and twenty acres of land for only ten thousand dollars."

I gave up. Calling the other numbers proved just as discouraging. When I told Cavit, he looked at me as though saying, "I told you so," but he didn't say it. Seeing my despondency, he urged me to keep looking. "Maybe you'll find something."

Our search went on for several years.

One day, walking through a lovely stretch of bosky lowlands known as Bluebell Swamp, we had noticed a wake on the still pond and soon saw that it was being made by a muskrat crossing the water. What a marvellously strong swimmer he was for his size! And he steered a perfectly straight line, being a better navigator then most human oarsmen. At last he gained the bank, alighted from the water, and clambered up a log. There he picked a place on which a spot of sunlight shone through the thick leafy cover, and in the welcome warmth he dried himself, preening his luxuriant fur with his little pointed snout.

And so we returned to Bluebell Swamp, hoping to inquire in the neighborhood about the ownership of the land and the possibility of buying a few acres. Yet even before we sighted the lake, an ominous growl greeted us. At last, we saw its source. A huge, yellow bulldozer was ripping the earth with its monstrous blade. It churned living land into grey, lifeless dirt. Along the water's edge, where I had often admired long-necked herons in their motionless stance, desolate mounds of stumps were now stacked, ripped out of the soil with their roots pointing toward the sky like torn veins stiffened in death. A monstrous billboard proclaimed ironically: "DEVELOPING 'COUNTRY ACRES'—HOME OF GRACIOUS LIVING."

More than ever I now felt the need for the refuge. If any wildlife were to be preserved at all in our increasingly crowded neighborhood, we had to act soon.

The sprawling brushlands where I had watched goldfinches and indigo buntings were fast giving way to cheap, split-level barracks pretending to be homes. Even bees and butterflies were getting scarce. Everywhere, it seemed, people were squandering their most precious heritage—the harmonious beauty of nature—for a shoddy kind of material "progress" that could never really satisfy their true wants and deepest longings. I though of Stephen Vincent Benét's story of Vasco Gomez, who died of starvation with all his gold piled before him.

I also thought of the rabbit family that used to hop leisurely around our lawn to nibble the dew-wet grass in the early morning. They had been murdered by hunters just outside our boundary. Nermin, my little girl, was inconsolable that no more rabbits came, and during hunting season, she cried at the sound of gunfire. A grey squirrel who had regularly come to our oak and delighted the children with his graceful gambols had been picked out of a tree by a passing gunman. He evidently wasn't interested in the squirrel. He just wanted to kill him, and he left the small, shattered body for the children to find and mourn.

I desperately longed for a patch of land large enough to let me protect all the animals who lived there and in which our children could enjoy their companionship without having them murdered almost before their eyes.

As if to underline my thoughts, as we walked sadly from what had once been Bluebell Swamp, a noisy little airplane swooped down over a nearby orchard, spewing a cloud of poison.

The following weekend we worked once again on Joe Maurer's farm. Joe had trouble getting competent field hands and Cavit, deskbound all week, wanted to help him. He enjoyed being out in the open. Besides, he insisted, "Farm work is the best kind of exercise." As for me, I liked working in the fields alongside Cavit.

During our lunch break at Joe's house, the talk naturally turned to the bulldozing of Bluebell Swamp and our disappointment at being unable to acquire the soggy bit of wilderness that had seemed just right for our purpose.

Joe's craggy face wrinkled with disdain. He was a tough, flinty farmer with no sympathy for sentimental fools who wanted to pay good money for bad land.

Though he welcomed our help, he didn't really understand why Cavit, a professional engineer, would want to spend his weekends as a farmhand. But, for reasons probably unclear to himself, Joe liked us. If we really wanted to make fools of ourselves, Joe figured, he'd help us.

"If it's swamp you want," he said, scowling over his dessert, "maybe I can show you some. I'll take you over in the truck."

We all knew Joe's truck. Its shock absorbers had long since succumbed to the deep ruts of his field roads. But it managed to stumble successfully over an erratic sand trail to a forlorn clearing along a large, neglected lake. Though less than five miles from paved road, the place looked primordial. Dead trees protruded ominously over what seemed to be haunted waters. Gaunt desolation rimmed the banks, and deep shade along the .overgrown edge contrasted sharply with the silver sunlight glistening on the water

Joe clambered out of the truck and took a large ax from the rattly tool chest at the rear. "Might be bears around here," he grumbled in reply to my questioning look.

I was troubled by his assumption that animals must be met with weapon in hand. The winter before, a small, black bear had indeed been sighted in an isolated hill region of northern New Jersey. He was sleeping peacefully in a tree. A farmer promptly shot the helpless animal, for which the local papers celebrated him as a hero. It nettled me to think that Joe, our friend, would have done likewise.

But my anger at Joe and his ax soon was dispelled in the excitement of exploring this unlikely spot.

Near the bank, we came upon a small shack and a tumbledown barn beside the pond. Faded curtains were drawn tight behind the cracked windows of the cabin, so we couldn't see in. But the decrepit condition of the place was only too apparent from the outside. The porch sagged and some of its broken floorboards angled upward like jagged spears. Half the barn roof had crashed down from the rafters, and smashed bottles and rusty beer cans surrounded the place like a beleaguering army. Yet despite the presence of all this trash and the predominant mood of decay, a kind of serene beauty inhabited the place. Great tall trees ringed the cabin and somehow gave the poor broken shack the aspect of a secret castle in the very depth of a great forest.

With Joe clearing the way ahead, Cavit and I forced our way through the buttonbush, sweet peppers, and rank swamp grass that had grown up all around the pond. Branches of maple, oak, magnolia, and wild cherry reached down into the wild profusion of undergrowth.

Untangling ourselves from the maze of greenbrier, we scrambled over fallen trees and came to a small clearing opening the view toward the pond. Without a word Cavit and I stopped, as if to savor it. The halting of our footsteps restored a deep silence that reassured a song sparrow nearby. Suddenly he began to sing.

Our reverie was interrupted by Joe's crashing through the underbrush. "Gotta be gettin' back," he said. "Thought you might like this place. Virginia Adams owns it. Maybe you can talk her into selling."

❄ ❄ ❄

Mrs. Adams treated us rather coolly. She was a rich, matronly woman with a rather stiff-backed manner, evidently in no hurry to sell anything at all. She asked us what we would do with the land. We told her our plans for an animal refuge. Her face registered disbelief and suspicion.

Crestfallen, I tried a new tack, counting on her feelings for animals. "I noticed the little elephant statues in your hallway," I said. "Are you fond of elephants?"

"Yes," she replied. "I'm a Republican."

We left it at that.

We were greatly encouraged when we discovered in roundabout ways that Mrs. Adams was making inquiries about us. Perhaps she thought that Cavit and I were a "front" for real estate speculators. This may have seemed a plausible explanation for our "crazy" talk about a wildlife refuge, and in my more mischievous moods I like to picture her surprise when she found out that we meant what we said.

A few weeks later she confronted us with an offer: "I wouldn't sell to a developer," she said. "But I like what you're trying to do. You'll have to take the whole parcel, though. Eighty-five acres."

The price she quoted was reasonable enough. But eighty-five acres was more than eight times what we had considered feasible. It meant a huge debt, even if we could raise the down payment.

Getting Mrs. Adams to sell had proved easier than getting Cavit to buy. True, he had been going with me to look at land and talk to realtors, but he had viewed these activities more as Sunday excursions than impending cash deals. As long as the land was unavailable, he felt safe. Now his bluff had been called, and he again retreated temporarily behind the newspaper.

His position, however, had already been undermined. Sooner or later, we both knew, we would jointly have to face the moral obligation I felt toward animals. We had already clashed on this point on several occasions. Each time, it turned out, Cavit came a little closer to my view—not as a matter of "giving in," but in the course of serious thought and honestly gained conviction.

It would be hard to trace what amounts to a spiritual development in terms of outward events. Yet one episode sticks in my mind.

We were traveling southward on Virginia's Skyline Drive on our way to visit relatives in Tennessee, when I noticed a bird at the side of the road. No sooner had I recognized the bird as a brown thrasher than he dashed across the highway. The car ahead of us whizzed over him, striking him down, but fortunately not crushing him under the wheels. I could see that

69

the bird was still alive. He lay on his side on the hot pavement, his beak wide open, gasping for breath.

I hit the brakes.

"Don't stop!" Cavit shouted. "You can't stop in the middle of a four-lane highway!"

"I've got to stop," I said. "I can't leave him like that!"

"Daddy! The bird is hurt!" cried the children in the back seat.

"Go on! Go on!" Cavit shouted, his face darkening.

Yielding to his anger, I drove on. At the next turnout, Cavit, still grim-faced, ordered me to pull to the side. "I'll drive," he announced.

The children were crying in the back seat—crying because of the wounded bird and because of our quarrel. For a long time, we didn't speak.

Later, in the evening, Cavit calmly explained that we couldn't risk a rear-end collision for the sake of a bird. We had no right, he said to imperil our own lives, the children's, and perhaps the passengers' in the car behind us.

I explained, not quite so calmy, that I hadn't planned to stop on the highway. I would have pulled over to the side and then stepped out in the road to rescue the bird.

Cavit shrugged—that ancient gesture of the East that consigns everything to fate. All human effort, it implied, is but a futile sham.

Whatever peace may lie in such a philosophy, I

wanted none of it. For his grand philosophic resignation said: Let the bird die.

I flared up: "I'm ashamed I obeyed you!" I shouted at Cavit. It was a terrible thing for a wife to say to a Turk.

It hurt me to quarrel with Cavit, and I hoped my remark would pass from his mind. But a year or so later I learned that I had underestimated him. Though he had said nothing more about it, he had evidently done some thinking about the implications of our argument.

The first indication of the gradual change in his attitude came several months later. It was dinnertime and we had gathered around the table. Halfway through his soup, Cavit said casually: "This morning on the way to work I saw a baby bird on the road."

I watched the children's interest pick up. They still remembered our quarrel. An uncertain, anxious look appeared on Nedim's face.

"Guess what I did." Cavit glowered, trying to look mean.

"You just left him on the road, Dad," Nedim said, his toneless voice reproaching his father.

"Well, there was lots of traffic and I couldn't very well stop," Cavit admitted.

Tears started in Nedim's eyes and the girls looked crestfallen.

Cavit could no longer prolong the suspense.

"So I had to go on nearly a quarter of a mile, cross

the median strip, and get back to the bird in the other lane. But he was still alive when I got there. Every time a car went over he flattened himself against the pavement. The cars came so fast I hardly had time to jump out on the road to pick him up." Casually he dipped into the soup again.

"Oh Daddy! You did!" Nedim's face lit up. The girls screeched with happiness.

"Well, I picked him up like this," Cavit explained, cupping his hand over the soup spoon. "He held on tight and I put him under the bushes by the roadside. His mother was sitting in a branch, scolding me. I think he was a robin, just learning to fly."

A sense of happiness filled our room.

I think the experience of seeing the little bird united with his mother made a deep impression on Cavit, more so than any of my arguments. A short time later, another incident betokened his change of heart.

Again we were on the highway, this time with Cavit at the wheel. On rounding a curve we saw a wounded cat in the opposite lane. She was crouching low, cowering at the cars speeding over her. Before I could recover from the shock of seeing the injured cat, Cavit had swung the car onto the shoulder and was jumping out to run back toward her. While I held back traffic, he took off his jacket and gently rolled the cat into it, lifted her as if in a sling, and we took her to a nearby veterinarian.

As it turned out, the cat's pelvis had been crushed, and the best the vet could do for her was to dispatch her without further pain. I felt deeply saddened, yet wonderfully happy at the same time. As we left the vet's office I took Cavit's arm and said, "Thank you."

Again, Cavit shrugged. But now that shrug meant something different. It meant: I do what I can.

Maybe this explains something about Cavit. The man who once dismissed the whole idea of an animal refuge with the curt remark, "Animals don't pay rent," was now weighing the possibility of devoting all his resources to such a project. We talked about it for days, he stressing the financial folly of such an investment, while I pointed out that the refuge represented both a way of life and a moral commitment.

At last he said sourly, "We'll have to use the kids' education money."

And so, with my delighted assent, he robbed our children, hocked our future, and bought the land.

FOUR

It was too late in the season to rebuild the cabin before winter, and not until the following year could we start the job of turning the brokendown shack into a livable home. But meanwhile the cabin served as base camp for exploration of the forest and swamp that now were ours.

It was still warm, and everything was verdant. Skirting the pond, we made our way to the woods, where a dim path led along the shore and broadened out to a leaf-paved trail among the trees.

"They logged in here," I said, as we followed the road. "I can still see the tracks where they pulled the logs."

Farther on, our way was barred by an arm of the swamp, which reached in among the trees. The water looked black and treacherous, but the trail continued on the other side, so we waded in, coming out on higher dry land beyond. It was a fine grove of oak, maple, and pine, thickly undergrown with sweet pepper, laurel, blueberry, and dangleberry, with ferns underneath. Draped all through were the ever-present greenbriers, reaching up sinuously toward the sky.

At one point the old log trail approached the swamp's edge, and we looked out on a scene of devastation. The whole swamp had been full of cedars. Cutting ruthlessly, the loggers had left tops, butts, and worthless splinters, along with hundreds of broken-off stubs, saplings permanently bent over, and a host of rotting branches that had served as corduroy roads. Amidst this waste rose a few hesitant swamp maples, some small cedars on which green branches still lingered, and a mass of sedge and other marsh plants, thickly matted.

We pushed through tangles of greenbriers along the shore. "I hope we'll have beavers in our pond," I said. "Do you suppose there are any?"

Cavit was ahead of me, bending aside branches and reaching to foil the tough brier stems which grabbed at us.

"I'm at the dam," he called. Then, "Oh!. . ."

I came up to him, and we both stared at the dam. Dark water was falling over, and caught in the swift current was a dead beaver, his round furry body washed constantly by the rushing stream.

"There *were* some, anyway," Cavit said. "Hope that wasn't the last one."

We turned our eyes out to the somber pond, and looked across the expanse of lily rafts to the maze of dead trees beyond. Amidst their stark nakedness, far out, stood a huge pile of debris, heaped up in conical fashion.

"There's the beaver lodge," I whispered. "There *are* beavers here. Or at least there were." My eyes fell again on the dead beaver. "I just hope there's a pair of them left," I said.

The sun was setting, filtered through a black lace of branches. The mystery of the swamp both repelled and attracted me. Possession turns sand into gold, the old proverb tells us. And the sun lay like gold among the lilies, which had gone to sleep for the night.

As we walked back to the house, a crow appeared on top of a tall stub, and regarded us curiously.

"There's one crow, at least," I exclaimed. "A start on our wildlife."

"There may not be much more," said Cavit.

Indeed, we found few animals but plenty of shotgun shells. For many years, our woods had been a favored spot for hunters. I shuddered at the thought of the suffering that must have taken place. Our first step in turning a killing ground into a sanctuary was to post the land. We tacked up hundreds of "NO HUNTING" signs, not yet realizing that it would take far more than nails to make that message stick.

It occurred to me that I might restore some of the animal population of the ravaged land by stocking it. But I quickly dismissed that thought. I could have brought in a few quail and pheasant. But birds raised in cages do not readily adapt to life in the wild, lacking the benefit of having been taught by their parents how to live under natural conditions. To put cage-raised animals out in the open would be almost as cruel to them as to release them just in order that they be shot by hunters.

Besides, artificial stocking of animals can never duplicate the balance of nature. I wanted nature to find its own equilibrium with no interference from me. I wanted foxes as well as quail, otters as well as fish, and owls as well as mice. True, I realized that some species might never return, having been slaughtered to extinction by years of systematic killing. To this day, I have not yet seen a skunk or a bobcat on the refuge, nor a groundhog. The blind destructiveness of hunters and farmers has robbed us of these beautiful creatures.

A dirt road branching off toward the refuge from a paved highway a mile away was called Unexpected

Road. I never found out what accounted for the unusual name, but its allegorical overtones appealed to me. It somehow pleased me to think that our home and haven was to be reached by Unexpected Road, and Cavit and I decided to name our land "Unexpected Wildlife Refuge."

We still lived in our old house, but spent every free moment at the refuge. To our immense joy, we gradually discovered that, despite past ravages, the land was not so depleted as it seemed at first, and our constant walking and watching was rewarded by many meetings with animals.

Summer and early fall had gone. Most of the trees had been swept bare, and all along the woodland paths lay leaves crisp and crinkled for there had been no rain since they had fallen. Big flocks of robins lingered, feeding on chokeberries, persimmons, pears.

Water snakes still moved about, for the weather had not yet turned cold, but even the days were slightly chilly, and the snakes seemed sluggish, lying motionless on sunlit sections of the paths, and moving sleepily away when feet came near them or someone reached down and touched their tails.

A flock of fox sparrows came through, migrating; and brown thrashers, evening grosbeaks, and towhees arrived. I watched a brown thrasher eat an acorn. He hammered away like a bluejay, opening the acorn. When he flew away, and I came up to where he had been working, I found a round hole in the track which had served him as a forge.

One afternoon I encountered two pairs of wood ducks swimming confidently up the stream that feeds our lake. The males were marvellously colored, the gleaming emerald and blue of their heads set off by pure white markings down toward the throat. Red and white bills complemented this iridescent array of color.

I was particularly pleased that the wood ducks had found their way to Unexpected. The species has sharply dwindled in numbers partly because of the cutting down of old trees with likely nesting holes, partly because of hunting. I resolved to put up wood-duck boxes on poles near the bank to serve as their homestead—big boxes, about twelve by twelve inches with four-inch entrance holes. In my mind, I foresaw a flock of ducklings, creamy yellow and fluffy, with smoky grey backs and a dark stripe through their eyes.

My expectations were not disappointed: the next year, several pairs of wood ducks took up residence in the boxes. A friend of mine was fortunate enough to see a mother duck guide her ducklings on their first excursion in the water. She left the box, looked around carefully to make sure that all was safe, and then began calling. One by one, the little ducks climbed to the edge of the hole to look out, obviously afraid to venture forth into a yet unknown world.

But other ducklings, pushing from behind, eventually knocked the first one off his perch. He landed in the water upside down, but immediately righted himself and scrambled after his mother. The others, all hitting the surface with a slight plop, soon followed; and the mother duck, with visible pride, led them on their first swim.

My friend observed that, even on their first trip out, the little ducks proved themselves highly efficient as natural insect controls. They fed voraciously on mosquito wrigglers and picked up other small insects from the surface of the water.

How odd, that countless dollars are spent on controlling mosquitoes by poison while the bugs' natural predators, notably the ducks, are being ruthlessly hunted despite the growing scarcity of many beautiful species.

Another time, early in May, I saw the female wood duck look out of her house, then fly down almost vertically to drop with a splash in the water before her house. She began swimming frantically in violent dashes, as a mother bird will when protecting her young. "The babies must be ready to leave the nest," I thought, and settled myself on a stump to wait at a distance of about fifty feet.

The duck joined her mate out beyond the island and they floated slowly, not stopping to feed as they usually did. With infinite patience they floated ever nearer, circling, waiting, watching, side by side. Then they dipped together for food. They began feeding in the cove, and another pair joined them.

The air was heavy with dark blue clouds and the wind was rising, whipping the surface of the water into choppy waves. The wood ducks moved over to the east edge of the pond, among the weeds; then both climbed up on a stub and began preening.

While I watched them, a prothonotary warbler came flitting through the dark swamp behind them, glowing like flame.

An hour passed while I sat waiting. Above drifts of white dogwood, high in an oak a squirrel whisked along the twigs, stirring clusters of catkins as he ran. Redwings called "o-ka-lee" out in the pond; and flocks of swallows wheeled in the rising wind. It looked like rain. The duck had re-entered her box, and was again looking out, craning her neck.

I had to leave to look after the children, and when I returned, it was to find scattered egg shells and down mixed with dry leaves caught in the weeds below the pole of the duck house. The duck must have called her brood from the nest while I was gone.

One morning I was able to observe a determined if futile attempt by a roguish drake to break up a marriage. A female wood duck was quietly sitting on the shore with her mate when another male approached. The mated drake immediately took after the intruder, who retreated into the water but circled right back toward the female. Again he was intercepted by her husband.

Beak to tail, both jabbing at each other, the two plowed up the surface of the lake. From her low perch on a slanting log, on the shore, the female was calmly watching.

Every time the strange drake tried to get in close to

her, he was thwarted by her spouse. Between bouts both drakes dipped their bills furiously and batted their wings.

A mallard pair came sailing into the cove. As usual, they started after the smaller wood ducks, who normally hurried away. But this time the wood ducks, busy with their fight, paid no attention to the mallards. The bigger ducks soon ignored them and began to feed. Just then, a third male wood duck came swimming around the land spit. I expected a free-for-all. But he hopped up onto a fallen log and started preening his feathers, paying no attention to the squabble of the others.

At last the combatants separated, the intruder going off to feed by himself, and the protector, dipping his bill triumphantly and flaunting his crest, swimming over close to his mate. The female stepped down into the water and joined him. Peace restored, they started feeding side by side.

We learned in succeeding years that it was not enough to put up nesting boxes for ducks. It was also necessary to restrict occupancy. Instead of ducks, we often found screech owls, flickers, and squirrels making themselves at home. Occasionally, we even found a raccoon or a possum comfortably settled in. We didn't evict any of these tenants, but in the future we put three-foot-wide metal collars around some poles beneath the boxes to discourage four-footed climbers.

Wood ducks, mallards, black ducks, and ring-neck

ducks often came to the refuge, some staying over to nest, others only passing. They would stay until the water froze over, and then travel south. Sometimes I succeeded in luring the ducks onto the bank by throwing them corn. I remember a flock of wood ducks hopping onto the land and waddling toward me, picking up corn as if they were in a tearing hurry. Evidently they wanted the food, but felt insecure in my presence and in their exposed, beached position.

Images sometime stick strangely in the mind, and, despite all the ducks I have seen since, I still remember the two pairs who came to the refuge during our first weeks there at the approach of winter. I still can see them circling warily for a while, then retiring to a bend in the stream where they played in the water for a long time. The sun had risen and was shining rosily through mist. Whenever a duck dipped, water flowed like liquid gold off his beak, and when he shook his head, the drops flew out like glitter in the cold air.

Winter was lovely at Unexpected. Grey squirrels had grown white earmuffs and grey fur gloves. We could see them close as they came near the cabin to get food. Song sparrows and tree sparrows, white-throats and one fox sparrow all hopped near, picking up grain we scattered on the snow. With them appeared a company of grackles, blue jays, woodpeckers, titmice, and chickadees, and two pairs of cardinals.

A screech owl roosted in the woods. When we walked at dawn and again at evening, we saw him sitting silent and watchful in a birdhouse on a tall pole near the cabin.

The persimmon trees were loaded with frozen fruit, and became a feasting place for robins. The robins, three to six at a time, came early in the mornings, not making a sound when it was cold, but giving forth a few chirps on warm and rainy days.

Out on the iced-over pond, snow lay thick, and the skating was good where we cleared it off. Otters' tracks—a few steps and then a slide—crisscrossed the surface. Waterlilies, their stems and roots visible beneath the ice near the shore, looked succulent and edible. We saw occasional tangles, gnawed on, evidently brought up when the ice had broken. From along the east shore, covered with deep snow, a woodcock flew up. I was surprised to see him on a bitter cold day. Once I saw a muskrat swimming under the ice.

Then one day, when a warm spell softened the ice, I saw something that made my heart leap with happiness: sticks freshly gnawed by beavers! I knew then that my wish for beavers would come true. Evidently, they had taken advantage of the breaking up of the ice cover to foray out from their winter lodgings. Now I really longed for spring, hoping that I would then be able to see them. But even in my fondest expectations I could not have foreseen the friendship that was later to develop between me and the beaver family living in our pond.

During that first winter, we built a bird-feeder on

the open cabin porch. Not all visitors, however, arrived on the wing. Among the steadiest customers at the feeder, appearing daily at about the same time, was a charming family of five rats. All but one seemed young, agile, and graceful. No matter what people say, rats are beautiful, with their glossy brown fur on top, their pure white stomachs, and their little white feet tipped with fragile pink toes. I loved watching them, with their whiskers quivering and glinting in the sun, translucent ears moving constantly, pricking forward at each unusual sound. The old rat of the group was slow moving and hesitant. He looked partly blind. I called him Grampa. He was so tame—or was it just that his senses were dull?—that I could pet him.

Even the birds sensed his gentleness, and chickadees alighted fearlessly within a few inches of the rat's nose. And he never made a move to frighten them. He just kept eating, holding sunflower seeds, one at a time, in his delicate pink hands.

Cavit has the traditional attitude toward rats and wanted to get rid of them. But I asked him to let them stay. I enjoyed watching and sketching them, and in the wild setting I trusted that their proliferation would be checked by natural predators. Soon after, a screech owl took up his station nearby and the rats disappeared.

Rats have been accused of terrible things. It is certainly true that rats feed on human refuse. But why not remove the garbage instead of killing the rat? Man, suffering from crowded conditions in his cities, has picked on the rat as a scapegoat, and even drags the poor animal into politics with such slogans as "Rats cause Riots!" And children are brutalized by communities offering a ten-cent bounty for each rat tail. What, I wonder, happens to the rest of the rat?

Little Nermin watching the rats once called to me: "Look mother, they swim like submarines!" Indeed, sometimes they travel many feet under water. Occasionally a rat would take off and swim clear across the cove, a distance of thirty feet, to land on the island there and come back with a kernel of corn, salvaged from the mud.

"Here comes one now," Nermin would shout. "Look at the bubbles." A stream of bubbles would mark the rat's progress underwater. After gaining the shore, he'd give himself a dog-like shake, and then take his kernel home.

The forest floor was full of mice—voles, rather—furry and fat with short tails. I saw them humping through the snow or leaves, making their cautious way to the corn kernals. Each grabbing one, they would dart back under something to eat in safety.

One snowy Saturday afternoon, I was making brush piles for animal shelters in the woods. Snow sifted down lazily, and fell on an old stub where I noticed a woodpecker hole. There was cedar bark inside, and I thought it was an abandoned bird's nest. I pulled a little out to look at it, when all of a sudden a flurry of mice exploded around my hand. Some burrowed into the soft, shredded bark, some went out a side hole, and some darted over my hand and I don't know which way they went. I quickly replaced the fragment of nest and went away. It was good to see all that bright-eyed life, cozy in a warm nest while the snow fell soft and cold through the trees.

We didn't see a quail that winter, and only a single grouse. A lone rabbit left his tracks. A wood duck spent the winter in patches of open water below the dam. The swamp was filled with bird food—seed heads which were frequented by goldfinches and others all winter long. A kingfisher wintered in the swamp, giving an occasional rattle but not his voluble summer chatter. Over the woods now and then soared a red-shouldered hawk, and sometimes he gave a call.

One morning I watched six squirrels leaping from branch to branch, and climbing up and down trees. One fell more than twenty feet with a loud crack onto the ice, whimpered a little, then took himself off. Squeak, snort, whimper, chase. And in the middle of it all, a red squirrel sat calmly eating high up in a maple.

The red squirrel spied me. She came down in excited stages, chattering and twittering, jumping up and down with hind feet and then front, alternately. Reaching the base of the maple, she scurried over to the brush pile not twenty feet in front of me, from which she peered out, silent and suspicious.

Next to the brush pile, a group of juncos and sparrows fed. Now and then a junco hopped into a pool of clear ice water and took a bath.

I put food closer to me, and before long the red

squirrel sneaked out of the brush pile across the path, and appeared at the base of the pine tree next to me. She hopped all around me, chirping like a bird, and finally got a taste of corn at the far end of a log. Whenever I moved, she dashed away.

I named her "Quizzy." Day by day I put food closer and closer to me, and within two weeks Quizzy was eating from my hand. She always reconnoitered with birdlike chirps before venturing first onto my boots, then onto my lap, then into my hand. Before the winter was over, she was not afraid when I made a move, and she didn't mind other people's talking to her and feeding her by hand.

A wild animal must have ingenuity to keep living. Quizzy was adroit at selecting sound nuts; and she thriftily stored surplus food when she'd had enough. Whole nuts were buried in the forest duff; perishables like piecrust, bread, and shelled nuts she carried high up into trees and wedged into crotches where they would keep dry. Once I gave her a huge sweet potato, thinking she would gnaw on it while I sketched her. She started to drag it away. The potato was bigger than she, but she moved it. However, branches obstructed its path. Quizzy dashed ahead and chewed away interfering twigs along the intended way, then pushed the sweet potato with her nose and forefeet along the cleared path. Shoving and angling, she made her laborious passage, every little while leaping ahead to clear the way. It was hard work, but Quizzy's sprightliness and gay chirping made the task anything but dull.

All of us were busy that first winter making birdhouses. Friends pitched in too, especially one with a drill press, who helped us bore the holes; and by early spring we had nearly a hundred houses. Most were for bluebirds and tree swallows, but we had also made quite a few big ones for wood ducks, sparrow hawks, and owls. We did much of the work at the cabin, where we had installed a makeshift stove that kept us warm while cold winds swept off the frozen ponds or the snow fell silently in the woods. We stacked the finished birdhouses in the barn, eagerly awaiting spring, when we would put them up.

Spring came early, and it came with a bound. In mid-February the red-winged blackbirds were back; and by March mourning doves had begun to call, herons were fishing in sheltered coves, and ducks were quacking in the pond. The ice was melting; and pussy-willows had opened.

I sat with Quizzy one evening—I had fed her all winter—and drank in the heady wine of spring. Light was dimming and the sky turned a luminous grey. The woods was silent except for Quizzy's chirps and the rustle of voles searching timidly for corn.

Around me were the waiting trees, the pines soft and feathery, the oaks and maples stark and delicately twigged. Quizzy had eaten enough, but kept returning to store what was left. There was a wonderful smell in the air—damp swamp mixed with the perfume of swelling buds and future flowers. I thought of my work. Another winter was over, and all around me new life groped upward, growing toward summer fulfillment. My spirit leaped up, as a song sparrow sang goodnight.

It was still chilly, yet many nights we stayed out at the refuge, bedding down on the floor of the still-unfinished cabin. It was the time of year when we felt we had to get out there and be up early to hear, smell, and feel the changing world. Bird song seems especially sweet in spring; for it is not yet the daylong chorus, but rather the occasional sounding of individual voices, like small, cheerful prophecies of the summer to come.

One morning, just as a hint of light was beginning, and the moon was still bright, Cavit heard an owl hooting. He woke me and I sneaked out the door. There was a great horned owl, sitting high on a snag overlooking the pond, right in front of the house. He sat still briefly, then took wing, flying low over the trees into the swamp.

I was surprised to see him in the morning, for owls usually hunt at night; and I see them mostly near sundown as they awake from their daytime snooze. Then I hear them hoot in the early evening, and sometimes during the night.

To me, the hoot of the horned owl sounds curiously soft for such a big, fierce bird. But the cries of little great horned owl chicks, all downy white and helpless despite their beaks and talons, sometimes remind me of a catfight in progress. The call of the adult owl is usually a series of three to six hoots, uttered with a total lack of inflection, which give it a forlorn feeling in the dusky woods—"hoo, hoohoo, hoo, hoo."

We put up the small birdhouses in open places. The big ones, with the help of a ladder, we mounted in tall trees. Usually it was toward the end of March that the refuge perked up with new life. At night the pond would come alive with ducks swimming and quacking. Flocks of tree swallows wheeled over the water, feeding in the air. We heard a pied-billed grebe calling from the other side of the pond, and a great blue heron flew among the trees. By day, hundreds of red-winged blackbirds gathered in bushes over the water.

One March we had bitter cold weather late in the month. The insects which already should have been flying lay dormant; and I noticed that the swallows, who normally do their feeding in morning and evening, were now on the wing only toward midday.

Setting out multiflora rose bushes in an open strip beyond the pond, I saw a figure flying low toward me. He was feeding on the wing, in a zigzag fashion, at high noon. As he came near, I saw that he was a big red bat. He flew right over my head, dipping down as though curious about me, then fluttered on in the peculiar, erratic way of bats.

He flew a little beyond me; then he turned back, again swooping close to my head, where I stood in the bright noon sunshine, which was at last warming the air a little. He certainly acted odd.

The papers often carried warnings about danger of rabies from bats, and, though I was not afraid, the warnings did worry me a bit. He was flying so close, and right in the daytime! The only other bats I'd seen in broad day were hanging asleep in the woods or from beams in the barn.

Again the bat came toward me, flitting in an erratic manner, and almost grazing my hair. Why was he so interested in me? I felt a little uneasy, but my qualms gave way to my interest as a naturalist, and I stood still and watched him.

Back and forth, back and forth, the bat traveled, patrolling about a hundred feet of the open strip between the pines. The ribs of his "wings" showed like umbrella struts against the sun. He was a soft brown, with a wash of red on his head. As soon as I began studying him as a fellow creature of nature, I lost the suspicion that had momentarily gripped me.

Suddenly he swooped into the brush, and though I watched for him, I didn't see him fly out. Walking over, and looking close, I found him hanging at the tip of a bare twig of shrub oak. All around him were other such oaks with dead reddish leaves clinging to their branches. Why had he chosen a bare branch when he could have hidden among the leaves? Turning my head away, I let my glance sweep casually back over the oaks before me, and my eyes failed to distinguish the bat, even though I knew he was there. His camouflage worked, after all.

Moving close to the bat I noticed that he was hanging by one tiny hind foot, his thin, leathery wings neatly folded against soft brown fur. The wings covered his eyes, and their curved hooks pressed tight against the two sides of his chin. The back of his fluffy head rested against a stiff twig. When I stepped near he moved slightly, quivering his ears, but he did not uncover his eyes.

I rushed home for my camera. He allowed the lens to come within three feet, trembling slightly at the sound of my tread in the dry leaves. Each time the shutter clicked, he gave a shiver and his ears quivered. Whenever I came close to him he moved his hooked hands over his face in a protesting gesture and pressed his head back more firmly against his twig pillow. A frosting of pale tips gleamed on the dense, soft fur of his body. After several shots, I left him to his nap and continued setting out the roses. Before long he was again on the wing, flitting back and forth over my head in the brilliant sunshine. Apparently he was making up with a noon snack for the dearth of night-flying insects.

Later I reproached myself for the strange queasiness that first befell me at the sight of the bat. I had seen owls, hummingbirds, otters, and snakes—even a weasel—come close to me in harmless curiosity. Why should I have been afraid of an inquisitive bat?

Perhaps it was a remnant of common superstitions about bats that I unconsciously harbored. According to popular belief, bats carry rabies and bedbugs, and they get into people's hair.

The latter two notions are demonstrably false, though bats do harbor a parasite which resembles a bedbug. The legend of their flying into people's hair probably stems from the fact that the bat is guided by a sonar system—sound reflections of little squeaks too high for humans to hear. Since a head of hair tends to absorb rather than reflect sound, acting somewhat as does a stuffed pillow, the bat does not sense the presence of a hairy head as readily as that of bald one. As a result, bats tend to zoom up close to people with lots of hair, or thick clothing, only to turn away at the last moment.

As for rabies, Professor Roger W. Barbour, that avid bat student at the University of Kentucky, says that only about three to four percent of bats test positively for rabies, but that this percentage includes a vast majority of those no longer virulent. Even though long past the contagious stage, they still test positively.

Dr. Barbour assured me that "the little insectivorous bats seen flitting about at dusk are seeking insects for food, and present no danger at all to visitors."

I was delighted to learn in the course of my reading that, at least in San Antonio, Texas, bats were welcomed natural insect controls. Around the turn of the century, mosquitoes were breeding in the desert pools near the city, and since these pools were a water source for range cattle, they could be neither drained nor oiled. Meanwhile the mosquitoes presented an imminent danger of spreading encephalitis.

It then occurred to some Texas ecologists that bats, who eat hundreds of mosquitoes at a single feeding, might be invited for a permanent feast; and in 1911 a special tower was built near the ponds at a cost of nearly ten thousand dollars as a roosting place for bats.

The tower's designer, Dr. Charles A. R. Campbell, spent years exploring the caves where bats lived, studying their habits and noting what kind of interiors they liked. He designed the inside of the tower as a honeycomb of milled shafts corresponding to the fissures in a cave. The shafts were connected so that the bat droppings, all funneled into one bin, were sold as guano for a neat profit of five hundred dollars annually.

It had seemed at first, however, that the ingenious tower would be a great failure. No bats moved in.

Then, according to one account, a drastic event occurred to change the bats' minds. The Police Band of Mexico City happened to give a concert on the outskirts of town within earshot of some caves where thousands of bats were quietly sleeping away the day. No sooner had the band noisily launched a waltz called "Cascade of Roses" than the horrified bats swarmed out of their caves and fled northward over the desert. It never became clear whether their sensitive ears or their musical taste had been insulted, but the great swarm—an estimated quarter-million—finally settled in Dr. Campbell's tower.

Later, when insecticides came into vogue, the authorities switched from bats to chemical pest controls. I only wish that the city officials could have realized that bats, on the average, are a lot safer than DDT.

As the year ripened on the refuge, the woods grew full of flowers, and at last we saw our trees in bloom.

It was our first spring at the refuge, and we jealously counted each finding: a flicker and a cardinal; a pair of red-shouldered hawks; juncos and chickadees; many grackles and blue jays; quail feeding in the path; a song sparrow singing and the first phoebe. Small groups of grackles were strutting about on the grass, like visiting dignitaries.

The children reported each animal-sighting with breathless excitement, as if they had found a treasure. Cavit shared in the spirit of joyous discovery; and I felt a deep happiness in sharing with my family the kind of intimacy with natural things that only comes from direct observation.

As soon as the ground softened, we started digging the footings for an addition to the cabin. We could hardly wait to get the cabin ready for permanent occupancy. For a family of five, the space might be a little tight, even with the addition. But with all the outdoor space around us, we felt sure we wouldn't be cramped.

Earlier we had all pitched in to clean up the place,

hauling off endless loads of trash, containing an amazing proportion of empty beer cans, that the previous tenants had accumulated.

As Cavit dug the foundation of our future bedroom he uncovered baby turtles deep in the ground. Guided by instinct, they unerringly headed for the pond. Sorry to have disturbed them prematurely, we helped them down to the water. I watched one as he stood with feet partly submerged, looking about with perplexed curiosity. Having thus taken account of the world for the first time, he ambled into the water with an air of apparent self-possession and began to swim. His strokes were still feeble, but he evidently knew just what he was about. Then he encountered calamity. His shell caught against a straw on the water's surface, pulling him askew on his course.

The tiny turtle struggled valiantly to overcome the drag. His power was weak, but his persistence invincible. Ultimately, he overcame the straw and headed onward on his just-begun life journey. I sometimes think of the intrepid little turtle when I feel in need of inspiration and encouragement.

The biggest morale booster, though, came early in April, when I glimpsed the first bluebirds taking up residence at Unexpected. I stood in the cabin yard when I first spotted a small, sparrow-sized bird coming toward me from a long way off. As he drew nearer I recognized the rather fluttery, erratic flight typical of bluebirds. As he alighed on a nearby branch, I was able to verify his identity by the vivid

97

blue back and brick-red breast with a fleck of white near the undertail. I also recognized him by his distinctive way of sitting on the branch, slightly bent over, giving a round-shouldered appearance.

"A BLUEBIRD!" I shouted, though there was nobody to hear me.

He took wing again, dipped into one of the birdhouses along the bank, and then flew away again. It was almost too much to hope that he would find a mate and come to stay. But the very next day, I saw a pair of bluebirds near another one of the houses I had put up. Evidently they were setting up housekeeping. I watched them for a long time, flying about the house, uttering their soft, warbling calls whose melody to me holds all the beauty of life.

FIVE

I COULD hardly wait to meet the beavers. Ever since I had spotted their tracks on a winter day warm enough to lure them from their lodge, I had anticipated my first encounter with them as eagerly as I had awaited the arrival of bluebirds. I had always loved the looks of beavers—their round, furry shape, suggesting their

99

gentle temperament; their endearing waddle; their inquisitive noses adorned with long whiskers; and that curious broad paddle of a tail.

I thought that I would have to contain my eagerness until late spring, for during the cold season beavers do not often venture forth from their elaborately constructed dwellings. But to my surprise, I saw the season's first beaver while the pond was still frozen over. He was swimming beneath a thin sheet of ice, trailing bubbles that were caught under the frozen surface and marked his path like a string of pearls. Uncommonly large lungs and livers allow beavers to remain submerged as long as fifteen minutes, and the one I saw under the ice didn't seem at all worried about being temporarily cut off from the surface. He calmly pushed himself forward, using a kind of frog kick, the webbed feet of his hind legs making efficient paddles.

In other ways, too, the beaver is adapted to underwater life to a degree astonishing in a mammal. One can only think of seals, or perhaps of whales, for comparable mammalian adeptness under water, but they lack the beaver's competence on land. The beaver's heartbeat slows during a dive to conserve oxygen. His blood vessels constrict to limit heat loss. His nose and ears are closed in submersion, the latter being equipped with special valves; and the eyes are protected by an extra set of transparent lids that act like diving goggles when the beaver plunges down. In sum, the beaver is superbly adapted to his environment.

Rhyme rather than reason is responsible for the stereotype concept of the "eager" beaver. At any rate, I have rarely observed beavers to be in any particular hurry about anything. When left undisturbed, they usually move about in a very leisurely, relaxed way. Even when they are hard at work cutting down a tree, they take frequent rests from the exertion of whacking away at tree stems with their long, sharp teeth. I have watched beavers working for hours, but never very long at a time. In between, they eat snacks, or they may just sit resting or carefully grooming their fur.

The beaver I had seen swimming under the ice finally reached a point near the bank where the ice was melted. His head emerged; and after carefully reconnoitering the neighborhood for possible dangers, he gained the shore and waddled up to a spot where perennial moss provided him with a comfortable hassock.

He was medium sized, as beavers go, being about four feet long and weighing perhaps fifty pounds. But his compact, chunky body conveyed an impression of great muscular strength beneath the soft, furry coat. In my imagination, I pictured the beaver's prehistoric ancestors, the Castoroides, who weighed as much as eight hundred pounds. What splendid, powerful animals they must have been!

Sitting on his moss pillow, the beaver began his toilette. He tucked his tail between his legs to that it protruded in front of him. That way the tail conveys a special oil from glands located at the rear, a deep-

101

yellow liquid, which the beaver dabbed on his fur for waterproofing.

This oil, called castoreum, was once as highly prized as the beaver's soft warm coat. Supposedly castoreum was even better than snake oil for curing all human ailments. Trappers did their best to tout that notion, and greed feeding on ignorance led to a cruel carnage of beavers wherever the white man debauched the American wilderness. Significantly, the first great American fortune, amassed by John Jacob Astor, was blood money made from this wholesale slaughter.

At its height around the middle of the last century, Astor's Hudson's Bay Company alone bought about 153,000 beaver skins per year. The great naturalist Ernest Thompson Seton estimated the total number killed by man as a half million annually. A fur-trapper working in the Bitterroot Mountains between the Missouri and Columbia rivers reported taking ninety-five beavers in a single morning, then catching sixty more the same day.

By 1900, almost all the beavers in the United States had been killed and only small regions in Maine, Minnesota, and the western mountains still retained a few survivors. Only then did a few farsighted people awaken to the threatening extinction of the species, and they established sanctuaries and planted beaver pairs in areas where they had been exterminated.

It is evidence of the beavers' intelligence that they adopted countermeasures against man's recent invasion of their ancient realm. Early explorers of this country described beavers as daytime animals. The horrors wrought upon them by man seem to have prompted beavers to change their whole way of living. Now they usually come out only at night. In many locations they do not even dare to build their comfortable lodges—presumably for fear of attracting human attention—but instead live furtively in holes in the bank, like desperate refugees from the human species. But when they are left completely undisturbed for years, as at Unexpected, they regain confidence and work in daylight or loll in the sun, luxuriating like bathers on a sunny beach.

Much of the literature on beavers has been written from an exploitive viewpoint, discussing the value of their pelts, the flavor of their flesh, and their supposed benefits or harmfulness to man's economic endeavors. Almost nothing is said about their charm as friends and neighbors and the great interest they hold simply as creatures of remarkable intelligence and resourcefulness with distinctly individual personalities.

Our state conservation departments occasionally attempt to dispel foolish notions about the beaver's destructiveness. One writer in the publication *Arizona Highways*, commenting on the beaver dams as natural irrigation and flood control devices, declares outright: "Beavers become the very nucleus of wildlife conservation." Too often, however, state agencies continue to stress the purely economic organizations which are a source of revenue. In my opinion it would be better for both people and beavers if these agencies forgot economics and simply tried to tell people about the delights of beaver-watching.

I am fortunate in being able to share these delights almost daily, for the beavers in our pond gradually lost their shyness and now let me and my family come close to them.

As soon as we learned to tell them apart individually, we began naming them. Greenbrier and Whiskers were the senior members of the clan, and nearly every spring we happily counted some young ones, among them Fuzzy Face, Fluffy, Goldy, and Brownie. But it took a long time before the cautious beavers were convinced that it was safe to come near us.

After my first encounter with the beaver swimming under the ice, beavers rarely appeared in daytime. At night, I could occasionally see them swimming, but whenever they sensed my presence, they signaled danger by slapping their broad tails on the water and quickly dived out of sight. In the hope of observing them, I once sat quietly at the water's edge for an entire spring night, but the reward for my vigil was only the sound of distant gnawing and a rash of mosquito bites.

Toward mid-April that spring, we rowed at evening to a beaver lodge up the stream where we had heard beavers gnawing. Anchoring the boat by grasping a tree, we waited in silence, hoping to glimpse a beaver coming out for the night. The sky got darker and darker, and nothing stirred at the lodge. Disappointed, we were starting for home when suddenly there was a splash ahead of us, just around a bend of the winding channel, and turning the corner we saw a beaver swimming swiftly back and forth up ahead. He dived with a mighty splash. Soon he appeared farther along the channel, and as we approached, he dived again. He kept this up, always a little ahead of us, until we had followed the meanderings of the channel clear to the middle of the pond.

Before this, every beaver had slipped away before we could come close. But this beaver acted as though *escorting* us across the pond. We surmised his purpose. Beaver kits are usually born at that time of the year: there might have been youngsters in the lodge, and the father was luring us away from his family.

My later attempts to approach the lodge were always heralded by the beavers' warning signal: the sharp slap with tail on the water, and promptly all beavers would disappear from sight. Any unusual rustling, a loud splash, or even a repeated bird call is likely to set off the beavers' tail alarm.

In the water, the tail slap sends the spray flying, and on the banks it causes a mud-barrage, either of which would startle and discourage an enemy. After the tail slap, beavers plunge down into the water, thrusting their hind feet up into the air beside the tail as they dive in. Young beavers often have trouble managing a graceful thwack and dive, and I have seen them tip over backwards. But they improve with practice and soon manage to launch themselves without back flops.

The beavers' defense is very efficient against practically every natural danger. Only man's traps and guns find them helpless.

The lodge itself is rather like a fortress, buttressed with sticks and brush and cemented with mud which freezes solid in winter. The entrances are far down in the water below freezing depth. And while interlaced twigs spike the exterior of the lodge like a barrier of spears, the inside is softly furnished with long fibers shredded from wood or bark.

An astounding feature of this defense engineering are the plunge holes that often dot the banks of beaver ponds. Located sometimes twenty feet from the shore, they are the openings of underground tunnels, partly filled with water, leading into the pond from beneath the surface. If any danger threatens a beaver while he is foraging ashore, he does not have to run all the way back to the pond for cover. He just slips into the nearest plunge hole, leaving his pursuer to wonder how the beaver so suddenly disappeared. The openings of these tunnels are often well concealed by mats of brush or overhanging weeds, and the usual way I manage to find them is if I step right into one.

I had told our friend Merrill Cottrell, a noted animal photographer from nearby Millville, about our beavers, and Cottie promptly came out to Unexpected, laden with cameras. As we rowed toward the dam the beavers had built to raise the water level of the pond, the late afternoon sunlight, reflected from the water, shimmered on the overhanging branches and made it seem that the trees were trembling in the stillness. Suddenly we heard a beaver splash, but ripples on the pond were the only sign of the animal's presence. After a few minutes, the beaver suddenly emerged from beneath the water quite near us. I think it was the big one I had named Greenbrier. He took a long, careful look at us, and before Cottie could focus his camera, he silently slid beneath the water again.

As we waited for more beavers to appear, a green heron flew to a fallen cedar, alighted on it, and began to skulk along it. Raising his head, he stretched his graceful neck until it looked almost twice as long as in its normal curved pose.

Dragonflies, horseflies, and mosquitoes buzzed about us in the spring air, and delicate reflections of sunlit apple-green leaves enlivened the water. A wild dove flew into a gnarled pine stub, solemnly regarding us for a full minute.

A prothonotary warbler appeared from around the bend of the stream that feeds the pond. His effervescent song announced him long before he came into sight.

Suddenly the air was filled with frantic bleating as two less-than-half-grown wood ducklings ventured out into the water while their mother yelled from the bushes. The pitch of her voice rose to a frenzy as the young paddled about, their tiny bills opening to emit piping little cheeps. With great aplomb and complete unconcern, looking like two floating powder puffs, they turned upstream and paddled clear out of sight before their mother finally rushed after them.

At last the beaver reappeared, swimming toward us fast and confident, but slowing down as he came closer. He circled and swam to and fro several times, as if testing our reactions. A little while later, another large beaver, the one I called Whiskers, joined the company, and both of them came straight up the bank near us and started eating. Cottie at last got a few beaver pictures before Whiskers and Greenbrier returned to the pond and dived under a log.

Gradually the beavers were losing some of their shyness. Nearly every day I broke off some poplar branches, an acknowledged delicacy for beavers, and left them at the dam. Whiskers and Greenbrier came regularly toward evening to nibble on them. Greenbrier was still a little shy, and often stayed back if he saw me too close to the poplars. But Whiskers was getting quite chummy and would contentedly sit beside me after her meal to comb out her thick fur. At those times, I would talk to her gently. She listened gravely, now and then answering with a soft whine.

Despite his shyness, Greenbrier allowed me to watch him at work. One of his projects was a dam near the outflow of the pond to raise the water level. The other was a large beaver lodge near the lake shore.

He was very busy. Every evening he went out to cut down trees and to transport materials to the building site. In his mouth he carried sticks, diving on the way to gather a big armload of mud. Then, rising to his hind feet, he stalked up the steep side of the lodge he was building, carrying a big bundle of mud and sticks. He looked like a little man struggling to get up the stairs with an outsize grocery bag.

Sometimes he had a log too big to carry, and he shoved and tugged at it until he got it up the side of his building. His manner suggested that he had a firm plan in mind and knew exactly what he was doing. His effort was unhurried but persistent. Like an experienced craftsman, he seemed to be working at a comfortable, natural pace, stopping occasionally for a short breather or a snack, but always going right back to the job.

Cottie and another photographer friend, Alfred Francesconi, guided me to the point where I was ready to make my own first attempts at animal photography with an old Graflex. Among my first projects was a photographic day-by-day account of Greenbrier's home construction. At dusk I would wade out toward the beaver lodge, holding my camera firmly with both hands and cautiously feeling for a safe footing at the bottom of the pond. Once my foot caught on a jagged root, tripping me. In trying to save my camera, I leaned too far backward, lost my balance, and fell into the water with a huge splash. Somehow I managed to keep the camera dry by holding it above my head.

No sooner had my own splash subsided than Greenbrier gave several mightly tail thwacks of his own, signaling alarm at my unusual behavior. As I lifted myself out of the water, I spoke to him soothingly. He had long since learned to recognize my voice and soon calmed down and continued his work while I sat watching him, gradually drying out.

Whiskers sometimes pitched in on building chores. Between them, she and Greenbrier seemed to have worked out a highly efficient division of labor. Greenbrier would often go ashore to fell trees while Whiskers worked in the water, pushing and tugging the materials toward the building site or bringing up mud.

Sometimes I observed Whiskers and Greenbrier swimming together in playful circles, diving and splashing, now and then touching noses. Greenbrier often gave a low murmur, and Whiskers voiced a gentle reply.

In felling trees, Greenbrier displayed all the caution of an experienced woodsman. Working hard with his long, sharp teeth, he cut a ring around the stem. Then, as the first creak of the trunk announced the imminent fall of the tree, he jerked back and stood still for a while, watching the trees and listening. Then, very cautiously, he approached the tree to take another bite. Now the tree began to lean. Again the beaver jumped back, his speed and agility quite different from his usual slow motion. Little by little, bite by bite, Greenbrier brought down the tree. Just before it fell, he rushed to the water and dived in, apparently for protection. After a while, he surfaced and circled the tree that was now lying with its crown in the pond. Then he came ashore, inspected his own work at the stump, and promptly began stripping the bark and snipping off branches from the fallen tree.

Many people believe that beavers use their spatulate tails as trowels in their construction work. This has never been substantiated, and my own observations give no support to this notion. Beavers use their hands and noses to pat mud into place, and sometimes I have seen them walk upright on their hind legs while carrying building materials in their hands. To jam a stick into place, either in dam construction or lodge building, the beaver grasps the stick firmly with his teeth and then, turning his head sideways, jerks his head vigorously downward to jab the stick in. He may repeat this several times with the same stick if necessary, each time grabbing the stick a little higher up, so that the whole length of the stick is gradually pushed deep into the structure.

The tail, however, serves an indirect function in the building process. When long sticks have to be hauled through the water, their drag often makes the beaver yaw. In that case, the tail, serving as a strong rudder, is used to compensate for the yaw and keep the beaver on course.

Another widespread misconception, repeatedly disproved by my personal observations, is that beavers and otters are enemies and do not peacefully occupy the same waters. One winter morning I saw an otter come up from a hole in the ice. I sneaked along the shore and got within about seventy feet of him. From behind some bushes I watched him as he turned his little head with the bristling moustache this way and that, like a man with a tight collar, pulling strips off the fish he had caught, much in the manner of a fish-monger preparing filets, and ate them. After finishing his meal, he let himself back into the water, tail first.

I stepped from among the bushes and was now in full view from the lake. Half a minute later the otter returned with another big fish. I think he saw me. At any rate, my yellow raincoat would almost surely have attracted his attention. He seemed undecided about what to do, started to eat the fish, but was apparently uneasy and turned around several times. Finally he retreated into the water, taking his fish with him.

It was shortly after this encounter that I had another great experience. For the first time in my life I heard the song of the winter wren, so delicate that you have to hold your breath to hear it. It came from islands near the beaver lodge where overturned roots and fallen trunks invited the wren to perch—a tiny little flute-like whistling, unbelievably gay and yet haunting.

After that, I had many occasions to observe the several otters living in the pond, and they never failed to delight me with grace and playfulness. Most of the full-grown ones measured about four feet in length and were some ten inches in height, and they had foot-long tails. Their motion is seal-like, liquid, flowing, and suffused with an ease and elegance that any dancer might envy. Except when they are dozing in the sun, they are rarely still, and their quick lively motions add to their charm. When he swims, the otter undulates like a porpoise, and, unlike the beaver, he always seems in a hurry.

Once I saw two otters vigorously swimming side by side. Seeing me, they stopped at once. But otters have an unquenchable curiosity, and the larger one couldn't resist the impulse to inspect me more closely. Circling and snorting, he swam toward me and then back while his mate retreated beneath overhanging bushes and waited quietly. I got a fine look at the big one as he reared his upper body out of the water and surveyed me, giving a loud snort that, to me, sounded like a distinct expression of dismay. He then returned to his mate, and the two slipped underwater together and headed upstream.

Like the beaver, the otter has suffered much from the infinite cruelties of trapping and in many areas is almost completely extinct. Their persecution is continued at the behest of fishermen, who believe that otters will deplete their trout streams. Recent observations, however, indicate that exactly the opposite is true. Without otters to catch the slower, less agile fish, the stream's trout population often becomes subject to fatal epidemics. As a result, where otters had been trapped to protect the fishing, the fish generally died of disease. So subtle is the balance of nature that it sustains the seeming paradox of the predator protecting his prey. I can only hope that the knowledge of these marvellous inter-species adjustments will become widely known among fishermen before their ignorance exterminates both otter and trout.

During the summers, I made it a habit of going out to watch otters in the early dawn. I would find them at about six in the morning, passing lazily through the water to a sunny patch of shore where they would sun themselves in the cool morning light.

Once I witnessed the encounter of two different otter families. The two groups, one consisting of two adults and two young otters, the other a lone parent with two young, approached each other swiftly. I was surprised at their lack of caution, remembering what I had read about the supposed fierceness of otters. When the families finally met, they rushed toward each other with eager nose-touching and signs of delight. Next the babies began wrestling together playfully and playing tag while the grown-ups gamboled about, showing off with splashing dives and fast wiggling runs through the water. This continued for several minutes. Then the two families separated, departing for opposite ends of the lake.

I continued to watch the group nearer to me and saw that the youngsters continued to play, two of them approaching a big stump from opposite sides. The first one to reach it clambered to the top and looked at the second with a challenging expression. What followed was a game of "King of the Mountain" in which they tried to push each other off the stump. The second otter climbed up, gave mock battle, and drew back in pretended defeat. Then the otter on top slid down from the stump to join the other one in further play. I stood on the shore for a long time, happily watching otter pups at their games among the half-submerged roots of the stump, and following them with my eyes as they swam farther away and at last disappeared around a bend.

With otter-watching in the morning before the children went to school, and beaver-watching before supper, our days at Unexpected never lacked excitement. Cavit, I, and the children usually went out singly to make our observations. Going in a group would have alarmed the animals. Every day at dinner-time, we would tell each other what we had seen. But the most thrilling event of our first years at Unexpected was yet to come.

I noticed that Whiskers was getting fatter at such a rate that I could no longer attribute her growing girth solely to the poplar feasts. I began to suspect that Greenbrier had something to do with it.

One day she stopped coming for her daily dinner. For a whole week I worried about her. At last she came back. No longer did she look like a furry blimp. She had regained her former shape, which by contrast seemed almost svelte, if that term can ever be applied to a beaver. Her breasts, the upper set located between her arms like those of a woman, were full of milk and pink nipples peeked out through her fur. Her manner seemed changed, too—reflecting what I took to be her joy in motherhood.

I resolved to find the beaver kittens, and hoped that Whiskers would not mind a respectful visit. In the evening, I waded out to what I thought was her lodge, sinking up to my knees into the soft mud, pushing aside tangled bushes, and threading swamp grass. The lodge looked dry and deserted.

Glancing downstream I saw a beaver swimming slowly, and something caught my eye beyond. There, built around a clump of trees, stood a huge pile of sticks, chinked and plastered with mud still fresh and soggy. A new lodge evidently had been built that spring!

The beaver did not shy away from me, so I assumed it was Whiskers and that her kits must be inside the new lodge.

Next day I sat down on the root of a big cedar just across from the lodge and waited. Half an hour later, Whiskers came from upstream and disappeared into the lodge. From inside I heard the mewing of the beaver kittens. Then, with the water swirling about the entrance, two baby beavers popped out. They swam around a little, awkwardly, tipping from side to side, their fur fluffy and buoyant. They looked less than a foot long, with tiny paddle tails. Soon the babies went back in, mewing excitedly.

Day after day, I came back to watch, always sitting quietly, reading with a small pile of poplar twigs at my feet. Sometimes I came at noon, to find Greenbrier at work. When he saw me, he swam swiftly back and forth, circled, and sometimes slapped his tail. I kept very still. Greenbrier began to calm down. When a week had passed, I could come to the lodge, sit down slowly, and not trigger Greenbrier's slap. Whiskers, of course, knew me too well to become alarmed and accepted my presence here as she did at the dam.

One night four babies came out. Water stirred around the lodge, and bubbles rose. With a "bloop-bloop," a baby appeared, floated along, and dived gracefully with a preliminary tip-up just like his parents. He came to the poplar, whining and trying to eat leaves. Three others appeared. Dark tails. Golden faces. One of them was a blonde with dark honey fur. They were about a month old then, still awkward and hesitant in their movements. They ate clumsily, holding the poplar twigs in delicate hands, tussling over disputed sticks with vexed whines. Sometimes one would drop his twig, then examine his empty hands in a puzzled manner.

Whiskers came out and swam cautiously over, nudging the babies aside and putting herself between them and me. She looked at me long and searchingly, then turned away and swam upstream. The babies clustered back at the poplar, less than a yard from my feet. Whiskers didn't even turn her head. It was then that I knew she had appointed me baby-sitter. But would her husband approve?

The next day Greenbrier saw me there with the babies and began to swim excitedly back and forth. He slapped his tail several times in quick sequence, which is the signal for a major calamity. Two of the little ones dived in with tiny slaps of their own, but two others, farther away, continued swimming and playing. Greenbrier swam to them, circling fast, and I expected him to shepherd them into the lodge. But he did no such thing. Coming back close to me he stared up intently, snuffing the air, his tail quiet. For at least a minute we looked each other in the eye. Then Greenbrier turned, swam over to the log which is one boundary of the pool, dived under, and paddled calmly on upstream leaving me alone with his youngsters.

I felt responsible for four precious lives. The red sun was just an hour from setting. The horned owl might fly by at any time and try to carry off one of the kits. Would the babies, naive and vulnerable, be easy prey? My muscles tensed, I was prepared to throw myself across the water to shield the babies if an owl came by.

On one of these nights, a horned owl did come, sweeping low along the creek toward the east, silent as death. He passed over the beavers and alighted on a dead tree not far down the stream. From there he watched me and perhaps decided I was too big to tackle. He flew away. When the sun went down the moon was already high, shining through the cedars beyond the lodge. Its light gleamed on little circles and wavelets churned up by the playing beaver babies. A bat flew overhead with tiny cries. Mosquitoes hummed. Should I go home before the parents came back? No. A baby-sitter does not leave her post.

Whiskers came just then, and her young ones hurried with eager cries to meet her. Swimming straight for the lodge, the mother led the four. She tipped up, dived under, and they followed, leaving a glitter of bubbles in their wake. From inside the lodge came a chorus of moans and whines, and soft mewings, as the babies settled down to eat. As the sounds became softer, I rose up, stiff from my long vigil, and splashed back through the swamp toward home. The dark was sparked with fireflies and alive with singing toads. A whippoorwill called. I felt that a great honor had been conferred upon me by Greenbrier and Whiskers in entrusting me with their children.

After this, I could hardly stay away from the beaver lodge. Almost every day I waded out to watch the little beavers playing. One of their favorite games was climbing up steep banks. At first their balance was very precarious, and if one beaver kit accidentally bumped against another, they'd both topple over and fall into the water together with a loud plop.

Practicing dives was another favorite diversion, interspersed with squabbling among the youngsters. Splash-plop-splash—what fun! Sometimes the kits amused themselves by wrestling, and when they became so boisterous as to disturb the older beavers, the parents would remonstrate with warning hisses.

When they were very young, the little beavers had trouble just sitting up. While eating, daintily holding their ilex twigs in their hands, they'd sometimes try to sit up too straight and fall over backward. Once I saw a little beaver falling on his side, but this didn't faze him at all. He had managed to hang onto his stick and kept right on eating in prone position, like an ancient Roman.

Within a year, the little beavers were nearly half grown and distinctive enough in appearance and personality to be individually named and recognized. We were particularly fond of one who was bolder than his brothers and sisters and whom we christened Fluffy. He was the first beaver kitten audacious enough to climb into my lap.

Cottie came to the refuge often to make a pictorial chronicle of my beaver family.

One evening he waited with his camera focused on a fresh pile of poplar I had prepared for the beavers along the bank of the lake near their lodge. Soon a small dark beaver head popped up among the lily pads, a dripping body emerged, and as he waddled ashore we immediately recognized Fuzzy Face, a year-old kitten.

But Fuzzy ignored the fresh food pile on which Cottie's camera was focused and set off for a bunch of old branches directly behind and inaccessible to Cottie. There he quietly munched away, to Cottie's growing frustration.

Shortly afterward, a bigger beaver whom we had named Wise Guy—possibly from an earlier litter— emerged rather briskly from the water and waddled toward Fuzzy Face in a definitely bullying manner. The two beavers exchanged some irritated comments in high-pitched voices, and Fuzzy Face fled, bumping into a leg of Cottie's field chair as he ran off.

Meanwhile Wise Guy was hogging the poplar, holding his food in one hand while he gestured gracefully with the other and extended his little finger in the manner of a Victorian lady holding a teacup.

Fuzzy surreptitiously crept back to shore and waited. After Wise Guy had finished and gone, Fuzzy returned to claim the leftovers.

Soon afterward, Fuzzy Face became sick. He grew visibly weaker and sometimes stayed huddled in one place for hours. His condition apparently encouraged a predator to take a bite of him. We found him one day atop the lodge, his tail bitten through and bleeding, and his body wasted to the bones. He let Cavit come right up to him and pet him.

We didn't know how to help him. Who could advise us on beavers? I called Fred Ulmer, the curator of mammals at the Philadelphia Zoo.

"It could be almost anything," he said, "perhaps some kind of infection. I really don't know what you could do."

"Would it help if we kept him in a cage where the others couldn't pick on him? Give him plenty of food?"

"Yes, that might help. They may be ostracizing him because of his sickness—driving him out of the lodge—a measure to shield others from disease. At least you could protect him so he can feed undisturbed."

Grey clouds hovered, making dark come early and

121

we felt the chill of rain in the air as we searched for Fuzzy Face. We had prepared a special feast to restore his strength: dog food, fresh strawberries, and fresh-cut poplar boughs.

"Maybe he's there among the reeds," Cavit said. We looked through the reeds, moving slowly along the shore. We peered into clumps of steeplebush, button-bush, and blueberries and among the tangles of green-brier vines. Then at the falls, I saw him, his face wedged into the sticks of the dam as if making a last effort to reach shelter. Fuzzy Face was dead.

We buried the little beaver behind the barn. For my younger children, it was a lesson in death, which is also a part of nature. For me, it was grief at the loss of someone very dear and a reminder that all of us living ones are highly perishable and should be cherished while there is time.

SIX

Men have their language and they have their music. With animals, it seems to me, music and language are one.

After the cottage had been refurbished and we took up full-time residence at Unexpected, I would often step out briefly between household chores to walk quietly and listen to the voices of the creatures who shared the refuge with us. I never failed to be astounded by the expressive variety and musical character of animal sounds. The warbling of a robin in springtime rain, the gabble of wild geese flying over in fall—such familiar voices are just a sample of the infinite animal vocabulary, of which human beings have noted only a few words.

The blue jay, for example, is widely maligned for his raucous screech. When the blue jay is near human dwellings he is on guard against cats, dogs, and our own unpredictable actions, and he is apt to shriek loudly and persistently. If we walk in his woods, he may warn family and friends that we are there. But sit quietly in the woods, hidden by brush, and listen to blue jays at ease. They talk softly to each other in a variety of low tones. And the hushed warbling of a blue jay song is one of the sweetest sounds in nature. A mother blue jay at the nest speaks with great tenderness to her young.

Why should we judge a blue jay's utterance by his yells of anger or fear? Do we rate a woman's voice by her occasional scream of terror, or rather by the tone of her gentler conversations?

The crow is another bird whose voice is widely presumed to be unpleasant. But such an opinion, I feel, can only be held by people unfamiliar with the full scope of the crow's varied language.

Ernest Thompson Seton, the great naturalist, once coded the cries of a crow leader by means of musical notes on a scale, and he found that each series of notes held a special meaning. My experience confirms his discovery. Our pet crow Billy taught me a lot of crow talk, though not the whole language by any means. His wild cawing when alarmed was in sharp contrast to dovelike coos he gave when bowing his head and fluttering his wings in loving communication with friends. Nestling beak-to-cheek he murmured gently in people's ears. And he prattled by the hour while engaged in solitary play.

Billy had his own distinctive vocabulary, as has had each pet crow we have known. In the wild, crows laugh heartily among themselves, scold, and speak softly, and many of their sayings are quite different from the "Caw" usually associated with their kind.

The starling, a rollicking extrovert, whistling at girls and calling out boldly, is sometimes accused of being noisy. Yet he is quite reticent about his true singing. Have you ever heard the starling sing his own song? It is pitched so low that only an attentive ear may catch the sound. It is enchanting.

Another study in contrasts is the brown thrasher's lusty spring music as compared to his autumn singing. In the latter season, his song still echoes the melodic pattern of his springtime call, but what once was a hearty, forthright tone is now muted to a whisper. Head cocked, and his white throat pulsing, he carries his lonely concert through the woods, changing his musical style to match the mood of the seasons.

One of the woodland's most charming singers is the

125

red squirrel. If you encounter him by chance, he will scold you in garish tones, protesting your intrusion. But once you gain his confidence, you hear an altogether different tune.

Quizzy, the red squirrel with whom I made friends, very distinctly altered her language as her feelings about me changed. At first, she voiced only outraged alarm at the sight of me, but as she grew tamer, she greeted me with bird-like chirps that seemed to express recognition mixed with caution. With closer acquaintance, Quizzy became less cautious and more inquisitive.

Another red squirrel we called Fiery because of his flame-colored tail sometimes came close to the house. One cool April morning, as the sun streamed through budding trees, Fiery arrived to claim the nuts I put out for him. He ate his fill, and carried off the remaining nuts to bury them in the black earth. Every so often, he interrupted the strenuous labor of nut burial to wipe his face on the cool, green moss.

When all his nuts were safely stored underground, Fiery scrambled up the dead cedar against which I leaned and, on gaining the upper branches, jumped into the crown of a neighboring maple. His landing shook the branch slightly and sent red blossoms dropping down into the stream below. Looking up, I saw him high above me, reaching out his little arm after the sunlit flowers which he was eating for dessert. I marveled at the beauty of the falling blossoms. Suddenly Fiery began to sing—that lovely, tenuous melody of the red squirrel.

One of the most poignant sounds in nature is the rallying call of quail. Near dusk on autumn days, when the hunters leave the woods, exulting over their spoils, the leader of the quail covey calls the survivors of his flock—sometimes a pitiful few—with his haunting mournful call. It is a heart-rending contrast to the joyous "Bobwhite!" call of the quail in springtime. Of all the quail sounds, perhaps the most charming is the prattle of conversation between a mother and her chicks as they thread their way through the grass. It seems to follow a lively question-and-answer pattern, and to my ears, it is antiphonal music of the highest order.

I have observed a similar conversational pattern among members of an otter family. The duck-like quacking of the otters as they move swiftly through the water is different from their utterances at other times. Otters playing or sunning on the bank converse with different inflections, and an otter parent guarding her young often gives a snort to warn of an intruder. Trappers tell of otters screaming fiercely or snarling defiantly in the agony of a trap. I am fortunate never to have heard these sounds, perferring the memory of the happy chirps of little otters playing with their parents.

Over the years, my observations of animal sounds have convinced me that the speech of animals in the wild—as contrasted with that in the constraints of a zoo or of an unnatural laboratory setting—is far more communicative and differentiated than is realized. In this area as elsewhere, our knowledge of animals is still scant, and our ignorance is compounded by hallowed falsehoods. Animal lore is a stronghold of entrenched superstition. For example, much of what is told of the wildness or viciousness of certain species simply is not so. To a large extent, man projects his own aggressiveness onto animals, creating an entirely false conception of animal nature. The very words man uses to describe his fellow creatures—beast and brute—are defamatory. In watching animals and listening to them, with respect and a humble heart, one can learn the realities of animal life and free oneself from common preconceptions. The knowledge thus gained inspires a wholly new relationship with animals—one based on affection rather than exploitive cruelty. And the animals, in turn, can teach us again something that so many of us in the modern world have almost forgotten—the joy of being alive.

The time of long daylight enabled Cavit, after returning from his office, to join the children and me in our observations in various parts of the refuge. As we gained practice in being sufficiently still and unobtrusive so as not to frighten the animals, more and more different kinds disclosed themselves to view.

Once I saw a red fox, pale, rangy, and incredibly long legged, trotting across the sand near the bank. Three fuzzy cubs galloped after him. They were about the size of cats, but with shorter bodies. Their color was grey with dark markings. They tumbled over each other, nipped each other's tails, and trotted around while their father curled up to rest at the foot of a pine near his foxhole. Every few minutes, the father fox rose, anxiously inspected his children, and then lay down again, always in a different place.

This is not uncommon behavior for the male fox. He is a faithful mate and shares with his vixen the task of watching and teaching the cubs. He hunts food for the whole family and often risks his life in leading enemies away from the den. On another occasion when I had come near a fox den, the fox jumped up boldly right in front of me, then turned to walk, always looking back to see if I was following. Only after he had lured me a safe distance from the den did he dash away into the underbrush.

With their standup ears, the three young ones playing around the tree looked like collie pups, very droll and cuddly. After watching for about ten minutes, I started to tiptoe away, backwards. Though I placed my feet as noiselessly as possible and avoided all abrupt movement, I was betrayed by a crackling branch. The father fox turned and stared at me. Several times he looked away, but soon he leveled his gaze directly at me again so that I could plainly see his slant-eyed "foxy" expression. We were deadlocked by our glances, and all I could do was walk away quietly, hoping he wasn't too alarmed.

As I took the first step of my retreat, the fox jumped

toward the cubs with a sharp, squalling bark, incredibly loud for such a thistledown creature. The cubs scurried into the den, with the fox continuing to bark while I backed away.

Next day I sneaked again to the fox den. As I got close, the two cubs were romping in front of the hole. I saw the adult fox hurry off to the right. I thought he might have seen me, so I left. A few days later I saw the cubs again, playing outside their den, this time without a chaperon. They looked about six weeks old, still fuzzy, blunt nosed and short legged, but beyond the infant stage. The cubs shook themselves, flicked their ears against flies, and scratched their fur. They looked sleepy, and suddenly one gave a big yawn.

Their coloring had changed slightly since I had first seen them. Their infant grey was turning to buff, but the only hint of their future color was a touch of pale red between the eyes. They were very woolly, with white tips on their dark tails.

Watching them play was a delight. Sometimes they plumped down together, appearing to sleep, but they were soon up again. They tussled. One investigated a dead stick, reaching his nose way out to smell it. I noticed how perfectly they blended into the leaves of the forest floor, and the buff sand and stones of the mound. The cubs went exploring all around the den, and they held mock battles, tails in air. They leaped and gamboled in the leaves. After about fifteen minutes they went back into the den.

After this enchanting interlude I hated to leave. So I

stayed on to watch a squirrel noisily eating a nut with crisp scraping of his teeth while titmice called loudly and an ovenbird's cry burst from a nearby dogwood. Then the little brown bird with a chestnut crown sang as he walked slowly along the forest floor, now and again breaking his stride with a graceful hop of fluttering sidestep to catch an insect stirred up by his rustling gait.

A scarlet tanager sang in a nearby oak, a flicker yelled, and crested flycatchers gave their thrilling "Gre-e-e-be!" Toads still trilled from the pond, singing into the early summer as if to make up for time lost during a late spring.

I called Cottie about the foxes, and a week later he came and set up his blind about sixty feet from the den. The day turned cloudy, but the foxes came out and he got several photos. Among them were views of the father fox peering distrustfully from the bushes.

A few days later Cottie came again and settled into the blind before dawn. For nine hours he waited with the uncomplaining patience of all devoted naturalists, but no foxes appeared. At last, he went over to the hole to look down. A few scraps of rabbit fur and a handful of blue-jay feathers bore witness to an earlier feast, but there were no tracks to and from the hole, though recent rain had made the ground soft enough to bear possible footprints. The foxes had moved out.

I hoped the little foxes would not stray far, for I well knew the fate awaiting them beyond the boundaries of the refuge. Few foxes nowadays escape lingering death in a trap, or terror-filled pursuit by hounds to a brutal climax. Hunters say they hunt foxes because they eat rabbits. They also say they hunt rabbits because we'd be overrun by them if they didn't. This doesn't quite make sense, but hunters' logic readily resolves the ecology of fox and rabbit: shoot both. That leaves a net balance of zero, which is far from nature's balance.

In my fourth spring at Unexpected, I busied myself during most of May planting millet, buckwheat, soybeans, and sunflowers—plants that make excellent wildlife food. All around me was a glorious riot of birds. Tree swallows were swarming around the birdhouses we had set up. Orioles were feeding high up in the treetops and the sun was flashing on the male oriole's brilliant plumage. Wood thrushes, tanagers, and ovenbirds sang.

A visiting neighbor who owned a nearby farm objected to all this "Those birds will ruin my crops," he grumbled, pointing to a pair of tree swallows who were gracefully skimming by.

"They'd never touch your crops," I assured him, pointing out that swallows feed on airborne insects and scarcely ever set foot on the ground. "Actually they protect crops by reducing crop-eating bugs," I explained, hoping to ingratiate the birds with the farmer. "And they eat lots of mosquitoes," I added.

"Yeah," he replied, "but I've got chemicals for that."

As always in spring, motherhood was rampant. Everywhere at the refuge animals were being born or hatched. From April till the end of June, I could hardly stroll along the paths I had cut through the woods without coming upon heartening evidence of new life.

I remember one particular occasion when my attention was caught by the amusing sight of a quail pursuing a rather bulky blonde raccoon. Apparently the raccoon had disturbed the bird in the underbrush, and now the irate bird stalked after her, scolding incessantly. The raccoon did not seem overly alarmed and waddled on, stopping occasionally to look back at the bird. Whenever the raccoon halted, the quail advanced menacingly toward her. The raccoon expressed her disdainful unconcern by turning her back and resuming her walk.

Some sixty feet from this encounter, the raccoon climbed up the lower part of a big gum tree by the lake and disappeared into a hole in the trunk.

It was seven in the morning. I sat and waited for over an hour, watching the sun rise through the mist and feeling the air grow warm.

A mother black duck followed by a fleet of tiny ducklings swam away past the hollow gum, making small waves lap at its roots. A blue heron flapped slowly east, pursued by a fast-diving kingbird. Mourning doves approached on whickering wings, and fluttered about in the pines, not daring to come down for the corn I had scattered to entice them. Bluejays held long discussions in soft voices and skulked closer, dropping from branch to branch. From all through the woods came the voices of flycatchers, ovenbirds, cat-birds, and others, mingled with the scratching of towhees and the rustle of squirrels.

It was just as my wet seat began to ache and my feet grew numb that I again saw the raccoon in the hole. She looked at me from time to time, peered up when a plane passed overhead, licked her fur, and dozed. Right behind me was a swampy section where gnarled old gum trees and huge swamp maples made a fine living place for raccoons. I thought this raccoon was on her way home, and, seeing me, had ducked into the hollow gum to hide till I went away. But by ten o'clock she was still there, her furry back filling up the doorway. Occasionally she stretched and yawned, or looked out, blinking at the bright sun.

Starting home for lunch, I waded nearer the tree to get a good look. The furry back stirred, the raccoon drew in, and then I saw two lop-eared kittens in the hole with her. It was a mother raccoon, and the hole was her nesting den. Seating myself on a log ten feet away I sketched the kittens while they played. Their mother nursed them and groomed them with her tongue. Once she left by the back door. I couldn't see where she went. Returning, she halted just outside the tree and gave a wild, ringing call before entering, a strange, piercing sound I had never before heard. She entered her nest, picked up one of her babies, and stepped silently out the back door. Carrying him high, with his tiny tail just trailing the water, she waded away, not looking back. The other one, left alone,

134

whimpered loudly. His voice was squeaky as he gave forth heartbroken, screechy kitten wails. After fifteen minutes his cries gradually subsided; his head drooped and he fell asleep. The mother came back soon and took him away. Once she stopped to get a better grip on his scruff but she never looked back.

Only then did I realize the tragedy I had caused. Because of me, the mother had taken away her youngsters and left her house desolate. Now I understood the meaning of that curious piercing cry—so different from the contented whicker of the raccoons' usual conversation. I had heard the anguished lament of an exiled mother.

Though shaken by remorse, I could not contain my curiosity about the abandoned raccoon house. I looked inside the dim hollow and found it lined with soft shreds of cedar bark. The hole itself had been filled up with sticks and leaves until the floor was level with the bottom of the entrance. That was how I had been able to see the babies inside.

Shortly afterward, though, I saw another raccoon with young ones as I sat near the dam to watch Whiskers, the beaver who came to the cove near the cabin every evening to claim the poplar shoots I gathered for her.

Whiskers sat quietly, combing her fur, when the raccoon came out of the thicket right behind her. Two babies were tagging along playfully, but the mother raccoon turned her head and chased them back into the bushes. After the babies were hidden again, the mother came forward to eat the food I had put on the dam for raccoons.

After that, the raccoon mother came each night, often before it grew dark, to gather some of the coffee cake, peanut-butter sandwiches, apples, and nuts I laid out for her. But she was much more cautious than the beavers and never came close to me.

The raccoon and the beaver were quite curious about each other and often approached within two feet to sniff. Neither seemed afraid of the other, and they ate peacefully in each other's company. Since the raccoon cared nothing for poplar and the beaver did not fancy the raccoon's fare, there was no competition over food.

One of the rarest and most graceful animals I ever glimpsed at Unexpected was a red-shouldered hawk, soaring and wheeling against a blue sky. It is very seldom that anyone in the New Jersey farming area can see a hawk soar, for only a few are left alive. No laws were passed to protect them until it was almost too late, and even now the law is flaunted by gun-toting farmers who think that every hawk—even the small kestrel—is a danger to their chickens. Actually, the main foods for the kestrel, or sparrow hawk, are mice and snakes, in addition to grasshoppers in late summer. And how any hawk can endanger chickens that nowadays are mostly kept in chicken houses is a mystery to me. But logic seems to be no protection against guns.

136

Quite recently, I had a remarkable encounter with hawks. I got a phone call from Al Rehmann, a friend of ours who had put up birdhouses for purple martins in the outskirts of nearby Vineland. "There's a big bird living in my martin house," he said. "It's got a long tail. I think it's a hawk."

"Are there any martins in the house?" I asked.

"Sure. Three pairs. They live in some of the other holes. And we've also got sparrows and starlings. Did you ever hear of all these birds living in the same house with a hawk?"

The situation sounded incredible. "Mind if I come see?"

"Mind? Of course not. That's why I'm calling, hoping you'd come."

When I arrived, Al filled in the background. Early in spring he had noticed that some English sparrows were setting up housekeeping in one of the middle-floor apartments of his eighteen-room martin house. He did not discourage them, thinking there was plenty of space left for the martins. The next arrivals were starlings. They claimed the lower floor. Al still didn't interfere. A few martins came and took up residence. Others settled in another martin house some thirty feet away.

Then those strange big birds usurped the remaining quarters in the top floor and had apparently hatched a brood there. Al was greatly puzzled by these outsized visitors.

I set up my observation post in an improvised blind, arriving with stool, book, binoculars, lunch, and camera, and getting ready for a day's watch.

My first sight of the mysterious birds confirmed Al's suspicion. Indeed they were hawks. I identified them as kestrels. They had a two-foot wingspan and vivid coloring, consisting of a slate-blue crown, a conspicuous black patch on the side of the head, a chestnut body with black stripes, and a bright red-brown tail with narrow black bars.

According to popular belief, the kestrels should have ravenously pounced upon the smaller birds. There certainly were plenty of birds to pounce on. Martins from the neighboring birdhouse wheeled overhead, along with the sparrows and starlings, all busy with their own affairs. Yet the hawks paid no attention. They came and went, fetching insects for their young, without bothering any of the other tenants. The smaller birds, too, seemed quite at ease with them. I watched a male sparrow bringing a bundle of green grass heads to furnish his nest, quite unmindful of the nearby hawks. Then he and his wife added bits of straw and feathers to the decor of their home, and, after that job was done, the male seated himself on a perch outside his door and chatted with his wife.

Kestrels occasionally prey on small birds. But apparently they were adaptable enough to respect their neighbors in this particular situation. To me, the mixed ménage in the martin house was added evidence that, in their social adjustments, animals seem often more civilized than men. I called my friend Al Francesconi, a professional photographer, to document this unusual cohabitation, and his pictures were published in the *Purple Martin Capital News*, which is published monthly in Griggsville, Illinois, by the Purple Martin and Wild Bird Society.

As the aims and purpose of our wildlife refuge became more widely known in the neighborhood, we were occasionally called upon to perform Samaritan duties for animals in distress.

"Want a loon?" the voice asked on the phone.

"A what?"

"Loon. Found him in the snow by the highway."

The great bird looked pitiful when the man brought him in a cage borrowed from the SPCA. He was covered with gummy oil and could neither walk nor fly.

Even in his bedraggled state, the loon was a magnificent bird, about three feet long with a broad back looking like a mosaic with bits of white embedded in predominant black.

I spread newspapers in the bathroom and gathered towels. Cavit brought in turpentine and a dull serrated breadknife with a blunt blade. Holding the loon upside down, we book turns scraping with the knife and dabbing turpentine, ending up with Ivory soap and warm water. Then we put him in the bathtub to swim.

Throwing his head wildly he lunged with his beak and flopped about. After drying him, we cut small strips of supermarket fish, but he didn't want to eat it.

We put him back in the cage for the night. All this time we handled him with gloves, for his beak was like a spear.

Next morning Cavit held him and I poked bits of fish down his gullet, offering him a glass of water between bites. He put his head in and blew bubbles. A friend who had heard about Loony offered to get minnows, and next day he drove in with a pail full of them. They ranged from three to six inches in length. We had Loony in a big cage by then, and we were handling him with bare hands. He thrust out his rapier beak seemingly at random, but he never attacked our hands.

We put some minnows in his water dish and in less than five minutes he had eaten fifteen. The minnows went fast after that, and I had to buy three dozen a day. We kept trying to clean off more oil, and as it was gradually removed, he became more lively. His eyes were big and dark, a rich mahogany red, set close together. The gape of his beak extended under his eye. Mottled grey on top, his head and neck were white below, the feathers incredibly soft. Over his back and wing coverts the dark grey and white resembled a guinea fowl's plumage. The rest of his wings and his tail were dark grey, and his tail was edged with white. We never ceased marveling at his pale yellow toes, with the nails rounded, and his thin, flat legs covered with fine overlapped scales. He carried his feet outward in the water like a pair of oars. He seemed to enjoy the bathtub, swimming from end to end and darting after minnows.

Yet our bathtub must have seemed confining to Loony, who probably remembered the open bodies of water where loons often gambol about like otters, chasing and calling each other. Some observers report that loons often dive playfully beneath each other, with the diving one suddenly coming up to topple the upper swimmer, then dashing along the water, uttering his characteristic laugh.

I had read much about the loon's strange voice, his conversational hoots and honks that are said to resemble a dog's howl, and that strange haunted call of which nature writer Helen Hoover says: "I have never heard anything more sorrowful or beautiful . . . yet the mournful sound did not bring loneliness in its ordinary sense, but an acceptance of the essential and natural isolation of the human spirit."

I hoped that Loony, when he felt better, would sing to us. But all the time he stayed, he rarely made a sound.

We had had him just a week, when he suddenly stopped eating. He began to batter his wings and he grabbed at the cage wire. His throat made a rattling sound when he breathed. After a while he was quiet. Loony was dead.

"Maybe the minnows are poisoned by insecticides," Cavit suggested.

"Perhaps he was hurt inside," I mused. "After all, they found him by the road."

We had better luck with another large bird entrusted to our care—an osprey who had gotten stuck under a duck blind near the Maryland shore, where he was found by some boys, who turned him over to a game warden. "I'd hate to give him to one of those 'wild animal farms,'" the warden said. "So I thought of you folks and brought him here."

The great bird with his six-foot wingspread was nearly the size of an eagle. His white head was gleaming, and the black stripe through and behind his eye showed in striking contrast. Although there were no signs of injury, the osprey was extremely weak, apparently having exhausted himself in desperate efforts to free himself from his entrapment. He was scarcely able to stand, and his wings and tail were battered and frayed.

I was very anxious for him to recover, because these beautiful birds are becoming quite scarce, being killed by DDT and other chemical pesticides draining from the fields into waterways where they poison the fish that ospreys eat.

I made a hurried trip to town and bought frozen smelts. Cavit held him, with gloved hands, forcing his beak open so that I could poke slivers of thawed smelt down his throat. After each piece was placed far down at the base of the osprey's tongue, Cavit massaged the bird's throat until the fish was swallowed, then released his hold until the next morsel.

At first Cavit tried to handle him with leather gloves. But after assuring himself of the bird's docility, he worked with bare hands. We placed water, sand, and gravel in his cage, which was thickly carpeted with leaves from the woods floor. We left him for the night, our last glimpse showing him hunched and forlorn, still crouched on his bed of leaves.

But the smelts and a good rest brought about his quick recovery. The next morning he had regained much of the majestic bearing that makes these great birds such an imposing sight. He was sitting upright on his perch, measuring me with the most brilliantly yellow eyes I had ever seen. Set off by his black and white crest, these blazing eyes gave the osprey a regal aspect, underlined by curved black talons that studded his feet like oriental daggers.

As the osprey regained his strength, he became more recalcitrant about feeding. It was almost impossible to open his beak by hand to slip in the fish. Yet he would not of his own will eat the minnows I set before him in a pail. Perhaps the fright and frustration of being caged was causing him to stage a hunger strike. The fact that he spread his wings whenever I came near strengthened this theory. Yet I hesitated to set him free. I had no way of knowing whether he would be able to fly well enough to escape a possible enemy. Unable to decide whether it was wise to let him free, I left the choice to the bird himself.

I thrust a stick into the cage, and when he gripped it with his powerful talons, I carried him on the stick toward the shore. No sooner had he glimpsed the familiar landscape of sky and water than he spread

143

those enormous wings and with powerful beats heaved himself aloft. Swiftly, and without apparent effort, he flew over the water toward the woods, passing behind a screen of low trees. He seemed quite capable of taking care of himself.

For many days afterward I looked for the osprey but spotted only several green herons who had been following the otters through the shallows, hopping quite close to them among the protruding sticks and vegetation. Either they were picking up insects flushed by the otters, or they were intent on scavenging the otters' leavings.

One day, at sundown, a big bird approached from the western rim of the water. At first sight I took him for a large heron, but as he turned slightly, I saw that he lacked the heron's hallmark: no legs were stretched out behind him in flight. As he came straight toward me, I soon made out his hawk shape and white head with the black stripe across the eye. It was an osprey—perhaps the one we had nursed back to health. Of course, I couldn't be sure it was really he, but the great bird coursed over the pond for several minutes, often passing quite close to my head. At one time he banked his flight so that the lower one of his outstretched wings pointed down toward me, his gesture resembling the traditional salute of aircraft pilots. Then he headed for the far edge of the water, where dusk engulfed him.

We were pleased at the spreading reputation of the refuge as a shelter for animal foundlings. Of the many animals given to us, I particularly remember a quartet of winsome young possums.

A boy, about ten, brought them to the refuge—four helpless little possum kittens with pointed noses, with soft grey fur and pink toes.

"My father won't let me keep them at home," he explained. "Please can you take them?"

"Where's their mother?" I asked.

"Killed by a car."

That settled it, I warmed some milk and got a medicine dropper.

Three times a day I fed the orphans with warm milk, and a few days later they began to clamber out of their shoebox.

Forever seeking motherly comfort, they clung to sweaters and nosed into pockets. Young possums cling to their mother's fur while she travels around. They desperately needed a full-time mother, and I finally thought of one—a stuffed toy. They clutched at it with mouths, paws, and tails, and on going to sleep they nuzzled the plush with their little snouts.

The possum, our only North American marsupial, may have up to twenty young, born a few days after mating. The youngsters, each smaller than a honeybee, crawl at birth to the brood sac of the mother, where each attaches himself to a teat. Since there are only thirteen teats, some are crowded out. During the first week the babies may increase to ten times their original size, staying in the pouch until they are about five weeks old. Then they may climb out to ride on their mother while she searches for food. They drop off one by one, when ready, to make their own way in the woods.

The four possums had been with us a week when their teeth cut through and they started eating bits of cheese and apple. They were crazy about fruit of all kinds, but turned up pink noses at dog food and cereal. As soon as they got to eating solid food, they disdained milk, which they had just learned to lap from a saucer. At the end of two weeks they were installed, box and all, in an outdoor cage carpeted with dry leaves and furnished with a hollow log and a tree branch. They liked to play with the leaves, sometimes grasping one in the curled tip of a tail and carrying it around. When tired, they snuggled close against their stuffed "mother" and slept.

Already they showed typical signs of possum behavior. They used their long, rat-like tails to grip the tree branch, often suspending themselves by their tails like monkeys. Surprisingly, they did not "play possum," when frightened.

"Playing possum," i.e., pretending to be dead, is thought by many people to be a deliberate trick. I, however, incline toward the view, shared by many naturalists, that neither trickery nor deliberation is involved. Rather, the possum's prostration seems to be due to fainting from sheer terror. The latter assumption is more in keeping with the possum's placid nature and rather dim intellect.

146

I enjoyed seeing the little possums amble about in their characteristic slow shuffle, and was often reminded of an account given by the naturalist Era Posselt of her friendship with a pet possum named Dixie Boy: "Our relationship was so pleasant that I am tempted to say: if the ticking of your clock sounds lonely, but you have neither the time nor the inclination to do much catering, get an opposum."

The little possums soon proved their self-sufficiency. They became extremely restless in their cage, and, unlike other young mammals I had known, each seemed bent upon going his own way instead of enjoying fraternal play. As they grew older, their determined individuality asserted itself to the point of mutual hostility. They began inflicting bites on each other that were by no means playful. It was at this point that I decided to let them go. I set their cage out in a clearing and opened a door. They walked off quickly, without hesitation and without a backward glance, each heading in a different direction.

Even among people kindly disposed toward animals one often finds a marked preference for furred or feathered creatures, accompanied by indifference or even aversion toward reptiles and amphibians. To me, however, a snake, a toad, or a salamander with its rich, colorful markings is as beautiful as any creature; and, perhaps in unconscious compensation for the common human hostility toward these animals, I have always held a special affection for them.

Pete Davis, a friend of ours, knowing my liking for reptiles, brought two pine snakes to release at the refuge.

They were a male and a female, purchased from a dealer. He had kept them until the pregnant female laid her eggs. They were a handsome pair, complementary in appearance, the female very dark and the male almost white. Letting them go at the shore, we watched to see what they would do. Almost at once the male slithered into the water, swam across the cove, and disappeared into the underbrush bordering an oak grove across the little bay. The female moved slowly into a loose brush pile, where she stayed watchfully for ten minutes. Then she moved down to the water and took a long drink. Pete told me that snakes eat very little for a long time before egg-laying, and are famished and possibly very thirsty afterwards.

That same spring, on a warm, bright day, I found a pair of water snakes mating. Wrapped around each other, they writhed and nudged, and I saw them kissing each other on the mouth several times. When I came close, they both looked at me in apparent surprise, but did not run away. Feeling that I had visited them inopportunely, I withdrew.

Another time I spotted a half-grown water snake swimming around a small pool, head high, writhing and contorting. Twisting and turning, sometimes upside down, he thrashed all over the pool, tail sometimes flying in the air. One of the beavers, coming to me for a twig, ignored the writhing snake, swimming

148

right past him. The beavers seemed remarkably non-chalant about other animals crossing their path. One time, for example, I saw a beaver heading straight for a large, green frog who was lazing in the water. Rather than swerve around the frog, the beaver simply dived under. But he surfaced a moment too soon and the surprised frog found himself taking a ride on the beaver. He did not jump off but seemed bemused at crossing the pond on beaverback.

To return to the writhing water snake, the snake returned the beaver's indifference, and taking no note of him, continued his curious acrobatics in the water even though the wake created by the passing beaver sent waves splashing over the snake's head.

For half an hour the snake continued his contortions. He appeared to be feeding under the surface, coming up every five seconds or so for air. His movements were energetic and rhythmic. Sometimes he blew a bubble as he came up. Once he got tangled in a twiggy branch a beaver was towing and took a ride of several feet on the stick. When he dropped off he landed on the beaver's shoulder, then finally reached the water again, to resume his gyrations.

I puzzled at the persistent antics of the snake. His motions resembled those of a swallow feeding over water—graceful swoops and dives and sudden curves.

Then he came near me. Creeping close through the water, he regarded me steadily, camouflaged against a floating stick. Closer and closer he came, hiding under leaves, keeping most of his body under water. At two

149

feet, he stopped and looked right up at me. With my pencil I reached down and stroked the back of his neck, then put my hand near him. He seemed unafraid. After a while the snake turned back into the pool and went on with his graceful dance, which, I assume, was the lively pursuit of the myriads of insects hovering near the surface of the water.

The snakes most frequently seen at Unexpected include, in addition to the northern water snake, the black racer and pilot blacksnake, the pine snake, king snake, keeled green snake, and hognose snake. Also, we have milk snakes, corn snakes, a variety of garter snakes, and tiny worm snakes, who burrow in the ground and look like outsize angleworms.

It is a pity that so many of these harmless and graceful animals are killed on sight by people who assume that every snake is a mortal enemy. According to common belief, every water snake is a deadly "cottonmouth," and all the lovely mottled garter and hognose snakes are presumed to be "rattlers." And because of the milk snake's reddish coloration, he is mistakenly assaulted as a "copperhead." True, there are a few poisonous snakes in our precincts—perhaps one in a thousand—but even they will not attack except to defend themselves when teased or accidentally stepped on.

Time and again, people bring me bludgeoned and mangled snakes. "I killed him with a stick," they usually tell me. "He's a rattler, ain't he?" Their egos usually deflate visibly when I tell them that their presumably heroic deed was the cowardly killing of a harmless creature.

The prevalent attitude toward snakes is typified by a clerk from whom I was buying a piece of foam rubber in one of the nearby towns. Cutting off the length I wanted, he had trouble handling the slithery material.

"It's like a snake," he said.

From the way he said it I surmised what he thought of snakes, but I wanted to find out for sure.

"Do you like snakes?" I asked him.

"Of course not! Do you?"

"Yes, I do," I said. "I love all animals, and don't you think snakes are about the most graceful animals there are?"

"Ugh!" he exclaimed with distaste. "I hate them."

"Why?"

"They're vicious!" They'd as soon attack you as look at you."

"I think you're mistaken," I said. "Snakes rarely attack, and then usually only when provoked." "One attacked me," he declared. "Down on the beach. I was just walking along, minding my own business. He ran right after me!"

"What did you do?" I asked.

"I waited for him to pass by me, then I fixed him!" he said with evident satisfaction and a vengeful look.

I said nothing more, but when he handed me my

package, I asked: "If the snake was attacking you, how come he went right past you?" I only got a scowl for an answer.

At Unexpected we have, over the years, enjoyed the companionship of many different animals, and there is no end to the sheer marvel and wonder of looking at them. I have seen lovely spiders weaving their delicate webs or carrying tiny baby spiders on their backs. Colorful moths have hovered about the trees at night, silhouetted against the full moon. Deer and their fawns have looked at me with their large gentle eyes and flicked their tails as a cheerful farewell as they leaped back into the woods. Rabbits have raised their families right under our eyes, quail have paraded before us, and owls have serenaded us in the night. Geese have rested on our lake during their long journeys while others have decorated the sky as they flew over. Among the singers who make music for us, the frogs provide a full chorus ranging from the piping soprano of the spring peppers to the *basso profundo* of bullfrogs. Toads and turtles have enlivened our shore, and whole passels of ladybugs have staged colorful displays as they emerged from hibernation.

But I feel that I should pay particular respect to one animal, much neglected, to whom we owe a great debt—the earthworm. Without him, as Gilbert White puts it, "the earth would soon become cold, hardbound, sterile." Darwin showed that earthworms produce one and one-fifth inches of top soil in ten years and that about ten tons per acre pass annually through their digestive tracts to be enriched by secretions of enzymes, nitrogen, and calcium. Dragging dead leaves and other organic matter underground, they burrow to a depth of six feet, keeping the soil aerated and drained.

By preparing the soil that nourishes all of us, this humble worm is vital to the support of the whole magnificent structure of life. Yet it is he who is today the principal victim of the soil-poisoning effect of chemical pesticides. I should like to offer an affectionate salute to the valiant earthworm in the hope that he and all of us living creatures may long prevail.

SEVEN

PERHAPS I had been naive in expecting the surrounding towns to be delighted at having an animal haven in their midst. While most people subscribe to the principle that kindness to animals is a good thing, they rarely connect this idea with action of any sort. When I tried to explain that loving concern for animals

154

entails practical responsibility for their survival and welfare, I generally met with uncomprehending indifference.

A handful of people, however, seemed downright hostile to the notion of an animal refuge. In some strange, perhaps subconscious way, they feared any kind of animal and were uneasy about animals settling anywhere in the neighborhood. A few farmers were incensed that I might harbor creatures who would raid their fields. For a while, the only real appreciation of our efforts came from poachers, who considered an animal refuge an ideal hunting ground, the idea of shooting in a sanctuary being about par for the prevailing level of sportsmanship.

The first of many incidents occurred soon after we had posted the land with hundreds of signs proclaiming the terrain as a refuge. Within a week, some of the signs had been torn down or defaced by hunters furious at being deprived of their accustomed shooting grounds. The wooden backings on which we had mounted the signs had been hacked to pieces.

I felt my scalp prickle.

"What will we do?" I asked.

"Put them right back," said Cavit, his jaw set.

Fortunately, we had a supply of spare signs. One by one we replaced the mangled posters along the road, working late into the dusk.

Suddenly headlights glared at us and a car pulled up. This was what I had dreaded. But when it came, I was calm.

The United States of America is a country devoted to the principle of private property and willing to defend this principle nearly everywhere in the world. Yet right here in New Jersey it is difficult to repel armed men invading your land. They take it for granted that a hunting license entitles them to trespass as well as to kill.

The sullen hunter in the car did not take it in good grace when he saw us posting our land.

"Trying to keep it all to yourself, eh?" he sneered, leaning out of the car. "A private game preserve!"

I tried to explain the difference between a game preserve for hunting and a true animal refuge. But I failed to get the point across. Compassion for the hunted was simply not within the hunter's range of sympathy and comprehension.

"You mean you don't shoot them yourselves?" he exclaimed in puzzled disbelief. The clash of different outlooks evidently confused and angered him. Spinning his wheels on the dirt road, he whipped his car around and roared off. I had an uneasy feeling that we had not seen the last of him.

"Let's notify the local game warden," Cavit suggested. "Maybe he can help us guard the place. I suppose that's part of his duties."

Responding to our phone call, the warden came to see us. He was a pleasant, well-mannered young man who explained politely that he could do nothing to protect the refuge.

"It's my job to see that there's no poaching off season," he told us. "And I have to make sure hunting licenses are in order. But if anyone trespasses on your land, that's for the police to handle. You'd have to make a complaint, and sign a warrant for arrest."

"But aren't you here to protect the animals?" we asked innocently.

"Against illegal taking," he said. "I love to hunt myself. It's the good old American tradition, you know."

I felt like saying, "So is shooting Indians," but kept it in.

We were on our own. Public authorities were evidently unwilling to extend themselves in our behalf, and even the state conservation officers regarded our venture with apparent indifference.

Not until later did I learn why this was so. The state wildlife agencies depend on the sale of hunting licenses for much of their revenue. This tends to pervert their mission. Often they end up by encouraging hunting rather than wildlife conservation. They are pushed further in this direction by political pressure from gun clubs, gun dealers, and gun manufacturers.

To what extent "sporting interests" influence our conservation agencies can be gleaned from an incident that was once reported to Joseph Wood Krutch. An officer of a state conservation commission protested against allowing children to pet a young deer in a state park because "making pets of wild animals creates prejudice against hunting." Reportedly, he clinched his argument with the remark: "After all, guns and ammo are big business."

Hunting stamps, too, are big business. What a paradox that hunting is licensed and promoted by the very agencies entrusted with the protection of animals! But hunting licenses are a main source of income for wildlife agencies and they try to sell as many as they can. Since there is not enough public land to accommodate the hordes of licensed hunters, the authorities tend to look the other way when hunters encroach on private property.

All this raises the question as to the real purpose of the various national and state wildlife agencies. Do they exist to protect animals or to provide animals for hunters to kill? As far as I know, nobody in government has ever brought this question forcefully into the open. Meanwhile, the wildlife protection offices do little more than run a nationwide shooting gallery with living targets.

The issue gains political significance from the fact that every one of us is required to subsidize hunting through our taxes. As *The Saturday Evening Post* recently pointed out, "somewhere in the neighborhood of 25,000 public wildlife 'conservation' workers, state and federal, consume upward of a half-billion dollars a year mostly to make it easier and quicker for gunners to gun things. No other sport comes anywhere close to being so pampered and coddled."

The article points out that the National Wildlife

Refuge system sets aside twenty-nine million acres of public land for hunters at a cost of about thirty million dollars per year, of which only five million is raised from the sale of hunting licenses. The remaining eighty-five percent comes from general tax revenues, much of it contributed by people who do not hunt at all. The same is true at the state level. Obviously, there is a fiscal inequity here to which any taxpayer may rightly object.

The article states that "our national wildlife policy, almost totally dominated by hunters, has been disastrous. A few months ago, for example, the Secretary of the Interior published a list of 169 species of animals judged to be either rare or endangered; that is, they have come perilously close to extinction. . . . Hunters must be skinned of the right to use the forest and fields as if they were a personal preserve—a private butcher shop."

Every year, during hunting season, Cavit and I patrol the refuge constantly, Cavit taking his annual vacation at that time to perform this guard duty. Time and again we have confronted hunters within our borders, and while most of them left peaceably, quite a few were rather unpleasant about it.

"I'll shoot you!" a teenage boy shouted at me, when I surprised him hiding behind a clump of trees. He showered me with obscenities.

"Go ahead and shoot me," I said. "I'm unarmed and it will be easy." Fortunately, the boy had sense enough not to take my dare.

That same evening, Cavit and I spotted a hunter right beneath one of our NO HUNTING signs. To our surprise, the hunter immediately took the offensive: "Get away from here," he ordered. "You're spoiling my shot. This is private land. Do you know whose land this is?"

"I know whose land this is," Cavit said. "Mine. And I'm patrolling it. What's your name?"

"None of your business," the hunter replied, in defiance of a law that stipulates that trespassing hunters must identify themselves when challenged by a landowner.

There was a tense silence.

The hunter said slowly: "There *could* be an accidental shooting, you know. Or someone could touch a match to your place."

Then he retreated down the road toward the boundary of the refuge, but not before he had ostentatiously cocked his gun.

Soon afterward we had more tangible tokens of a hunter's displeasure. Returning to the cabin after a week's absence, we immediately noticed a broken window. As we came closer we saw that the door was peppered with bullets.

"They shot off the lock!" Cavit called from the porch. As we pushed the door open, a shower of glass fell about our feet. The house was a shambles, the furniture kicked over, the glassware broken, and my father's paintings ripped by shot. His animal pictures had been used as targets.

Aside from the paintings, our tools were the only valuables we possessed. But they had not been taken. Robbery evidently had not been the motive. More likely, this was the way in which disappointed hunters expressed their opinion of our enterprise. What, I wondered, would happen next.

The next day I had to leave the refuge to give a talk at a weekend campout of the New Jersey Audubon Society. Worried as I was about the assault on our home, it helped to meet like-minded, sympathetic people, eat good meals, and take walks in woods. But my mind was back at the cabin where Cavit stood guard with a loaded shotgun.

My fears were mixed with admiration for my husband. He had come a long way. The man who once refused to stop a car on the highway to help a wounded bird was now risking his life for the sake of animals.

From that time on, Cavit and I intensified our patrols, crisscrossing our woods. It was our second autumn at the refuge. The gum leaves were turning red, acorns falling from their cups, and duck tracks coming from the pond clear up to the steps in front of the cabin. The duck tracks were intermingled with those of squirrels and quail. I couldn't make a gun fit into this picture, and refused to carry one.

My only defense was faith. But my faith was a straw. When I pictured invading gunners, and me meeting them unarmed and helpless, I shrank. I prayed, "Father, forgive them, for they know not what they do." But did I really feel it? And if I could forgive anything done to myself or Cavit, could I forgive their murderous intentions toward the animals?

Rather than condemn hunters, I tried to understand them. I tried to talk with them, to learn their reasons and their feelings. If I could approach them with understanding rather than fear or hostility, I felt, perhaps I could help them change their attitudes.

Our own attitude also changed. Cavit decided not to carry a gun on patrol. After thinking about it, we reached the conclusion that people who don't believe in violence should not carry weapons. Sure, it was risky to meet the trespassers unarmed, but Cavit and I were willing to back our principles with our lives.

When we met hunters on our land we drew them into conversation, and, if they seemed at all responsive, invited them into our home.

A surprising number of hunters turned out to be decent, pleasant men. We gradually came to realize that the majority of hunters are not vicious moral morons, but are good people tragically misled by outmoded tradition and commercial propaganda. Most so-called "outdoors" magazines glorify hunting with a kind of "tough-guy" sentimentality that appeals to men's egos. As a result, these otherwise decent people come to feel that they owe it to themselves to go out and kill something.

We got along quite well with some of the hunters we asked in, but when the talk turned to hunting, all

162

too often their views and ours seemed to go past each other without ever touching on common ground.

Time and again we hear hunters say: "Why not shoot animals? That's what they're for."

I counter this with another question: "What are *you for*?" But this only draws blank stares. The idea that a creature has the right to exist for his own sake and to enjoy his life seems to be incomprehensible to many people. They cannot find it within themselves to respect another creature's right to live—regardless of "what he is for." That makes it hard to argue against murder.

Other men, speaking with the false piety often used in trying to justify something morally rotten, say that it is all right for man to kill animals because the Bible says God gave man dominion over animals. I point out that this may be a mistranslation and that some scholars believe the meaning of the original text would be better rendered by saying that God entrusted the animals "into man's keeping." But most people, at least in this country, believe that God speaks English; so the argument about translation does not convince them—especially if the conclusion is inconvenient.

Some hunters have told me that they really mean no harm when they shoot at animals. "It's just for fun," they say. Which brings to mind the unknown Greek poet who wrote thousands of years ago that "boys throw stones at frogs in jest, but the frogs die in earnest." It also recalls a statement about bird-hunting by

Sir Pierson Dixon, the former delegate of the United Kingdom to the United Nations. "I like this shooting thing," Sir Pierson says. "It's like the pleasure of hitting a ball."

Sir Pierson, as do so many other hunters, misses a point. Hitting a ball hurts no one. Hitting an animal hurts, even when the shot is fired "for sport," i.e., without personal malice against the killed or injured creature. Sir Pierson's evident inability to put himself in place of the bird, or to see the essential difference between hitting a ball and hitting an animal, has been described by Joseph Wood Krutch as a "dreadful uncomprehending innocence." It is precisely this kind of abysmal blindness to the suffering of others that I cannot seem to surmount in talking with hunters who insist that an animal is "just a target."

"If it's marksmanship you're after," I suggest, "why don't you shoot clay pigeons?"

Invariably the answer is, "That's not the same."

One element is missing: the kill.

Most hunters rationalize this point. They do not admit even to themselves that killing is what they really crave. They go to extreme lengths of self-deception, persuading themselves that hunting is noble, manly, and "necessary to keep the animals from overrunning us." At least one hunter I met was more honest about his feelings. "A buck with his tail full of shot," he told me, "why, that's the funniest thing in the world."

Whence comes this urge to kill? It may be that

some men's minds have not yet caught up with human evolution. They still need the atavistic thrill of killing their prey in the manner of their distant ancestors. This is understandable when one considers the time factors of human prehistory.

Men have dwelt on earth, paleontologists tell us, for more than a million years. Yet agriculture was "invented" only about ten thousand years ago. This means that for ninety-nine percent of his total time-span as a species, man has relied on hunting as his only means of survival. Possibly ten thousand years are not enough to break a habit so long ingrained.

But man's world is changing faster than ever and we must rise to the challenge of changed conditions. Now that man no longer has to hunt for food, there is certainly no excuse for his hunting at all. What possible place has killing for sport in a civilized, humane society?

Jean-Paul Sartre has characterized this state of mind to which killing is acceptable as "fear of the human condition." The murderous man, he believes, "wishes to be pitiless stone, a furious torrent, a devastating thunderbolt—anything except a man." Thus the tragedy of the hunted also becomes the tragedy of the hunter.

Relations between man and his fellow creatures have reached an unprecedented crisis in which—more perhaps through ignorance than malice—man assumes the role of a cancer in the tissue of creation. As the late biologist Rachel Carson puts it: "I truly believe that we in this generation must come to terms with nature, and I think we are challenged as mankind has never been challenged before, to prove our maturity and mastery, not of nature, but of ourselves."

Meanwhile, vast damage is being done. The extent of the present crisis is not yet fully documented, but a few startling facts are emerging.

The federal Bureau of Sport Fishing and Wildlife, attempting to estimate the dimensions of the continuous orgy of murder taking place in our country, added up the number of deer, elk, and other big game shot legally during 1964, then doubled the number to allow for animals killed by poachers. This is considered a conservative estimate, because many gamekeepers believe that the total poaching kill is greater than the legal kill. To this they added an estimate of the annual bag of the ten million small-game hunters in this country, figuring ten pounds of game per hunter for each of their 128 million "recreation days."

According to these figures, presented in the *U.S. Department of Agriculture Handbook No. 325, 1966*, on page 75, the total annual carnage comes to about one million tons of carcass.

That is how the Department of Agriculture expresses it. One wonders how much concern for the beauty and joy of living animals might be found among bureaucrats who think of the dreadful dying of countless lovely creatures as "tons of carcass." Indeed, the very language the hunter speaks is designed to hide the raw fact of killing.

The term "fair game" is a case in point. The notion of fair game implies two things: 1) The animal must have a chance to shoot back; only then is the game fair. 2) The animal and the hunter must trade shots by mutual consent; only then is it a game. So until the animals are equipped with firearms and willing to fight duels, hunting is merely assassination. To call it by any other name is to dignify murder.

The statistical gentlemen in Washington, in their survey of hunting, have also figured out the cost of hunted meat, which comes to three thousand dollars per ton. It's cheaper at the supermarket.

Primly the government concludes: "Obviously, the sportsmen buy fresh air and exercise rather than meat." I am all for fresh air and exercise. Something, it seems to me, must be wrong with our values or ways of education if we can't have healthful outdoor activity without bloodlust.

Seen in a larger perspective, man's depredations upon his fellow creatures are but part of his pervasive destruction of the total environment—his pollution of air, water, and soil. Man, it appears, is unique among animals in fouling his own habitat. In view of such penchants, the survival chances of our species seem yet uncertain. But beyond injuring his own kind, man is drawing his innocent fellow creatures into his own deadly predicament through the technical efficiency of his killing methods.

This problem has become acute only within the last two hundred years as the result of improved firearms.

As long as most guns were muzzle-loaders, haphazardly firing a single shot at a time, a sizable number of animals still managed to survive encounters with men. After all, until the beginning of the last century, it took minutes to prepare a single shot and required a wick burning in the midst of loose powder. But radically improved guns and ammunition, along with the introduction of telescopic sights have shifted the odds against animal survival. Moreover, the human population explosion puts ever-increasing numbers of hunters into the field while the animal population steadily dwindles. As a result of these trends, the level of overkill has been reached for many species: more are killed than can be replaced by the natural birth rate.

It is necessary to gather such data and to be aware of what is happening. Yet in my own mind I cannot reduce the anguish and tragedy of countless creatures to a set of statistics. A concept like "overkill"—a mathematical ratio between births and deaths—misses the main point of what it means to be alive. For life and death is always individual. Statistics deny and obscure this fact. There is no common denominator of existence. For life and death, the operative number is always one. That, perhaps, is what is meant by saying that man has a soul. I am sure animals do, too.

When I read the sad statistics of the long and cruel war man wages on his fellow creatures, I long for ways to atone for all the unknown suffering. My mind searches for the individual fate behind the numbers, wishing that my sympathy could make what is happening less terrible. When I speak of hunting, my memories are of crippled animals staggering into the refuge, bleeding from their wounds.

Despite all this, I am hopeful that in the future man will come to appreciate and cherish his fellow creatures. I believe we have reached a turning point in the relations of man to his non-human neighbors. My faith is based on several encouraging signs.

The first of these is the increasing popularity of animal photography as a substitute for hunting. In Africa, the camera safari is gradually replacing the senseless slaughter of the last large wildlife remaining on our ravaged earth. And here at home, I know several former hunters who have found the camera more satisfying than the gun, among them Mr. Cottrel and Alfred Francesconi, who have taken so many fine pictures at Unexpected. Several of these "converted" hunters have told me that stalking animals with the camera retains their favorite aspects of hunting—the pleasure of being outdoors and the opportunity to observe animals. In many ways, they say, the challenge of getting a good shot with a camera is far greater than the challenge of getting a good shot with a gun. It certainly takes skill and knowledge; and the refinements of modern photography, with its splendid cameras, choice of good lenses, and fast films, place in the hands of the camera hunter an instrument worthy of his skill.

The camera-hunter's ultimate reward comes through his closer observation of animals, giving him a vivid sense of the animal's life. How much richer is this reward than a mere carcass! In fact, some converted hunters say that once their curiosity about the living animal is aroused through photography, that dark urge to kill miraculously vanishes.

I believe that more and more hunters will undergo conversion from gun to camera. After all, the modern camera, offering the advanced features so essential to animal photography, is only a very recent development. It has not yet had enough time to let its challenge penetrate to the majority of outdoors men, who have yet to become aware that animal photography offers an enjoyable and fully satisfying alternative to hunting.

To make them aware, of course, requires an organized educational effort. It is in this area that much work remains to be done by all those who feel kindly toward animals. The idea that animals deserve our sympathy and protection is in itself quite new. The first law to forbid the wanton torture of animals was not passed until 1822 in England. For thousands of years prior, cruelty to animals was not publicly considered a moral issue at all; though, no doubt, there were always a few individuals who regretted man's inhumanity to animals. That killing for sport might be objectionable, as far as we can tell from literature, rarely occurred to anyone until the eighteenth century. For many people, it is still a revolutionary notion.

Fortunately, public awareness of the needs of

fellow creatures is steadily growing. Preservationist ideas are now getting wider attention than ever before. This, I believe, is preparing the soil for more intensive educational work on behalf of animals and for suitable political expression of such concern.

As part of my own contribution toward this educative effort, I have frequently spoken to audiences of all kinds, including children's groups. And it is in my contact with children that I find the most encouraging sign of all.

Nearly without exception, children have a natural fondness and genuine sympathy for animals and appreciation of an animal's beauty and joy of living. To me, this confirms that man does not have an inborn urge to kill, as is often claimed by those who take a pessimistic view of such related phenomena as hunting, warfare, and wanton cruelty.

How then, do our life-loving children turn into a race of hunters and warriors? Not by instinct, I am sure, but through persistent conditioning. Despite outward professions to the contrary, our society still places a high value on aggression and prepares our children for violence. The children's natural sympathies are thus gradually perverted and their spirits are hardened. As they grow older they learn that it is "sissy" to feel sorry for animals (or anyone else).

In thousands of ways—through television, movies, and other communications media—youngsters are constantly sold the idea that violence is fun. Why does our society tolerate and even encourage such mass brutalization? Possibly there remains, as a leftover from more primitive times, a widespread if unspoken belief that young boys must prove their manhood by killing, if not in war then by hunting.

Hunting thus fits the pattern of an aggressive, warlike society. Yet, fortunately, an increasing number of responsible people feel that such a society is as outmoded as hunting itself. If war is waged on the present technological level, the whole world will be wiped out. Warfare thus becomes meaningless.

Likewise, if hunting is continued on its present scale with modern weapons, the animal population will be wiped out. Hunting thus becomes meaningless in the same sense as war. It no longer has utility.

If mankind really has a sense of good and evil, here's a concrete problem on which to exercise that sense. It surely needs some exercise.

I believe that the growing recognition that aggressive attitudes are intolerably dangerous in the modern world will bring about a profound change in educational philosophy in the near future. Perhaps we may hope that coming generations of children will be allowed to retain their naturally humane and joyful disposition in later life, including their compassionate feeling for animals.

When this is accomplished, human society will at long last be ready for the great ethical principle expressed by the late Dr. Albert Schweitzer in the phrase "reverence for life." Not only will this make for happier relations among humans, but it will also set the stage for a new era in man's dealings with animals—an era in which man and animals can live together peacefully, and man can reap deep, life-enhancing pleasure from the company of his fellow creatures.

That time is not yet. As I write these lines, envisioning a happier future, guns are booming all around the refuge, for it is once more the hunting season.

Lately we have had less trouble with trespassers than before. Apparently, our constant patrolling has finally convinced the hunters that we are both vigilant and uncompromising. But while we have succeeded in reducing encroachment, we have no control over hunters who virtually ring the refuge, camping just beyond our boundary. The animals, of course, do not know where the boundary lies.

The other day, I saw a pair of gun-toting young men in their twenties just outside the refuge. We exchanged greetings, and a little conversation ensued. It developed that they had a deep love for the woods. I could sense it all through our talk.

"I wish I had a place like yours," one of them said in a voice full of yearning. "With all kinds of animals in it."

How well I knew that yearning. I felt genuine sympathy for him. But his next words made me sad.

"Then I could get my share of the game—whatever was in there," he said quietly, pointing with his gun toward the refuge.

Returning to the cabin, I crossed the upper end of

173

the pond, circled through the woods and again approached the boundary gate where I had spoken to the young man. Suddenly, I heard the boom of a gun and shot whistled through the leaves right in front of me. Another explosion shook the air. Then excited shouts: "I got him! I got him! A grouse!"

At almost the same instant, the bird sailed over me, failing in his flight, in obvious distress. He disappeared over the trees. A single feather drifted down to me. I picked it up and wiped off a speck of blood. Then my fingers began caressing the infinite softness of the token the dying bird had left me.

EIGHT

ONE morning, shortly after I had taken the children to the road crossing where the school bus picked them up, the phone rang. A secretary's voice announced that Nedim's teacher wanted to speak to me.

My first reaction was alarm. What has he done now? What possible mischief could Ned have gotten into. At last, the teacher came on the wire.

"Ned's always full of stories about your animals," she told me. "We thought you might like to come down here for assembly and tell us something about nature."

My relief at knowing that Ned wasn't in any trouble was matched by apprehension about what was to be my first public appearance. But the anticipated horror of facing an audience never materialized. The grade-school children were obviously eager to hear the "animal woman," and I, encouraged and warmed by their expectant faces, forgot all about my self-consciousness and simply spun out my account of Whiskers and Greenbrier and their beaver family, of the otters, raccoons, ducks, squirrels and bluebirds.

But as the hour drew to a close, I had not yet made my main point. It is one thing to tell about animals—children always respond to that. It's something else to awaken a sense of moral responsibility for other creatures.

With deliberate abruptness—to add dramatic emphasis—I shifted from my cheerful description of animal life to the shameful facts of animal death. And in closing, I told a little story:

In ancient times, I told them, there was a very wise man who was famed for being able to answer any question put to him. One day, a man jealous of the sage's reputation resolved to make a fool of him. He brought him a captive bird, holding it in his hand so that only the beak and tail showed. He asked the wise man, "Is this bird that I hold in my hand alive or dead?"

If the answer were, "Dead," he would open his hand and let the bird fly.

If the answer were, "Alive," he would crush the bird. The wise man thought for a moment, then replied: *"It is as you please."*

There was a moment of silence as I left the platform. I knew then that the children understood. The future of our animals lay in their hands.

Soon the principals of other schools in the area asked me to talk to their students. Apparently I developed a certain reputation as a speaker, for I received a visit from Mr. James C. McDonald, the former Chief of the Natural Areas Section of the New Jersey State Conservation Department. Would I give school lectures under the sponsorship of his agency?

I was wary. I acquainted him with my views on state conservation policies, virtually accusing him of misusing public money to subsidize hunting. To my surprise, he agreed with me.

"Raising animals in cages to have them shot by hunters is not conservation," he admitted. "I used to hunt myself. But now I want to preserve, not destroy."

"But you're part of the conservation setup," I objected.

"I've tried to get policies changed." He told me how he had proposed revoking the trapping seasons for muskrat, arguing how senseless it was to spend thousands of dollars for waterway weed control while at the same time killing off the very creatures who would keep the weeds down. "But no one listens," he added sadly.

"Don't you get discouraged?" I asked.

"Plenty. But I keep trying. Your lectures, too, would help. They'd be at least one step in the right direction."

He had won me over. I gratefully accepted his sponsorship, which enabled me to reach thousands of school children throughout the state.

Sensing the response of the children, I became convinced of the value of such talks. My experience with hunters had taught me that creating an animal refuge was not enough. A few acres of tenuous sanctuary could not assure survival for more than a handful of creatures who happened to chance on our land. Something more had to be done to stem the tide of killing.

Increasingly, I felt the need of speaking out in behalf of animals and to plead their desperate cause to those who destroy them either by direct assault or by unwitting connivance through ignorance or unconcern.

At this point, I also sought contact with adult groups, service clubs, church societies, and other organizations, hoping to stir their sympathy for animals. And, in a small way, my efforts have been successful enough to sustain my faith.

One measure of this success has been the gradual change in the attitude of my neighbors. After I had the opportunity to explain the purpose of the refuge to various community groups, the prevailing attitude toward me changed from the initial indifference and suspicion to sympathetic interest and support.

After I had addressed a civic club in the nearby city of Glassboro last fall, one of the members came up to me and said, "You know, we think of you as our Ambassador from the Animal Kingdom."

I was touched. I never would have described my mission so loftily, nor bestowed upon myself so magnificent a title, but it pinpointed what I wanted to be: a voice for those who cannot speak for themselves—a go-between to help make peace between man and his fellow creatures.

As might be expected, my welcome as a speaker was not always unmixed. At times, I had to contend with a certain amount of heckling. Once, as I was talking to a service club, a large man got to his feet, rudely interrupted me, and, as if to brush aside all my arguments as irrelevant, loudly proclaimed: "I shoot rabbits because I *enjoy* it!"

There was appreciative laughter.

I waited for silence. Then I asked quietly: "Do the rabbits enjoy it?"

This time the laughter was even louder. This saddened me. Evidently my audience thought I had made a joke rather than a point.

I particularly remember one occasion, near Christmas time at the beginning of deer-hunting season, when I had been asked to talk to a church group.

179

Counting on the Christian spirit, I anticipated a sympathetic reception. Yet no sooner had I arrived at the church than the minister began to taunt me: "I went deer-hunting this morning. Got myself a nice buck."

This caught me off guard. "*You* went hunting?" I asked in shocked surprise.

"Why not?" replied the minister. "We've got to eat and you have to kill them one way or the other." With a complacent smile, he proceeded to describe in gory detail the proceedings at a slaughterhouse. Perhaps he hoped to unsettle me before my talk. As it happened I was well aware of slaughtering methods, and it was precisely these things—deliberately hidden from the public by the meat-packing industry—that had long ago prompted my decision not to eat meat.

"I'm a vegetarian," I quietly said to the minister. For a moment, he was nonplussed. But he quickly recovered. Turning to the man seated beside him, he pointed at me with his thumb.

"I can't win with her," he guffawed.

He seemed to be gloating in his admission of defeat, trying to turn a serious moral question into a joke.

I resented this—less because of his obvious attempt to belittle me than because I felt that this man's manner was demeaning to his calling and his church.

When my annoyance subsided, I realized that he had provided me with an opportunity to stress a vital point: Christianity implies the brotherhood of all living things created by God. Standing under a large ebony cross, I began my talk: "Your minister tells me he shot a deer this morning. I am here on behalf of the deer. It is fitting that I speak under the sign of the cross, for I speak for creatures who suffer without guilt."

I do not know whether this had any lasting effect on the minister. I hoped that it might make him consider whether the Christian message of love and compassion was compatible with his murderous assault on innocent creatures.

Afterward I reproached myself for having been so censorious. As the minister's invited guest, I resented his affront. But this was no excuse for me to embarrass my host. Besides, I reflected, arguments seldom change attitudes. The best, perhaps the only way, to teach values is by example.

For someone convinced of the rightness of his cause, it is easy to lapse into a preachy, moralizing tone, and I keep trying to avoid this. I present my talks as a factual account of my work at the refuge, describing the animals who share our daily life. But I make a special point of correcting the many misconceptions that are often given as reasons for persecuting animals.

Particularly I argue the case for beavers and otters because periodically there is talk of allowing these rare and lovable animals to be trapped again. I try to arouse public opinion in favor of the beavers and otters. I point out that beavers, far from doing the damage for which they are so often blamed, are great preservers of natural resources. They are nature's own hydraulic engineers who help regulate the water economy of entire regions. Beaver dams prevent flood and erosion by slowing the flow from the headwaters of a river. By impounding water where it may seep underground, beavers contribute to a high water table, providing insurance against the effects of a drought.

In my talks I quoted this passage from *The World of the Beaver* by Leonard Lee Rue III: "Beavers fully understand the problem of water levels and their control . . . They have been known to divert or to channel springs and streams to the main pond (created by their dams) in order to maintain a higher water level."

To illustrate this point, I told my audiences of an incident—one among many—recently reported by the University of Arizona. In one Arizona valley, beavers had been trapped for their fur until, quite recently, they became extinct in that area. As a result the beaver dams went unrepaired and could no longer withstand the onrush of flood waters. Instead of storing the water of sudden storms in pools, from which it could infuse the ground, the water now rushed unimpeded through the brooks, and the formerly verdant valley has turned into desert.

I told of the rivers where all the otters had been killed. When none were left to catch diseased fish too slow to escape the otters' reach, epidemics spread among the fish until the rivers became barren.

I began a mail campaign to augment my speaking activities against the pending trapping legislation. I

182

alerted various humane groups, wrote to newspapers, state legislators, and the conservation department. None of this prevented the Fish and Game Council, composed of farmers, fishermen, and hunters, from decreeing an open season on beaver and otter. Incredibly, Mr. George Alpaugh, Chief of the Bureau of Wildlife Management, attempted to interest more young people in trapping—as an alternative, he said, to juvenile delinquency. Noting that trapping had changed in the past few years from being a "revenue sport" to an "enjoyment sport—safer than hunting but still with the thrill of the catch," Mr. Alpaugh said he believed it would be an educational adventure for the kids. "It will bring them into closer contact with nature," as he put it.

These cheerfully sanguine notions of New Jersey's Chief of the Bureau of Wildlife Management should be put in the context of a more recent article in the *New York Times*, which notes that "trapping, as it is usually practiced, is hideously cruel, inflicting hours of pain upon its victims before they die."

Of course, I protested the enactment of the new trapping laws. In reply I received a mimeographed note signed by Mr. Lester G. MacNamara, Director of Division of Fish and Game, assuring me that the trapping would be managed "in a responsible manner with scientific finesse." One wonders if Mr. MacNamara would consider it an act of scientific finesse if somebody trapped and skinned *him*.

I believe that true science is maligned when its

name is used to justify needless butchery. What, after all, constitutes "scientific" knowledge of animals? Cutting them open to explore their anatomy?

How does this principle stand up when we apply it to people. Take any nice stranger, slit his throat, and dissect him. After you have neatly laid out all his organs, traced his nerves and veins, and teased apart every strand in his muscles, would you be able to say: "Now I know this man?"

Yet this is precisely the way animals are described in so-called scientific books. As with people, we can really *know* animals not by dissection but only by admiring and enjoying the nature of their being, respecting their personalities, and being ready to share the world with them.

It seems a pity to me that biology is rarely, if ever, taught as a humane subject. Certainly the kind of laboratory dissection practiced in most schools is not likely to awaken compassion or love for animals. Granted, for students preparing for biological or medical careers, detailed knowledge of anatomy is essential—though at the undergraduate level even that could be taught from plastic models rather than animal cadavers. At that stage of their education, I believe that children would learn more about animals by watching a frog jump or hearing a cat purr. Whatever intellectual loss they may suffer from not poking about cadavers would be more than balanced by the emotional gain of contact with a living animal.

It was on this point that I had a quarrel with

Cavit—one of the few serious disagreements in all our years together. It happened when Nedim came home from school, saying that he did not want to dissect a frog. Having absorbed my own feelings about animals and having cherished the frogs in our pond, he was disconsolate. "They don't have to make a frog die for every student."

"Just tell the teacher you won't do it," I told him.

"What do you mean," Cavit broke in. "You're telling him to defy the teacher!" He turned to Nedim. "You do what the teacher tells you. You're there to learn—not to tell the teachers what you will or won't do. Don't ever disobey a teacher."

"What good are frogs when they're dead?" Nedim asked.

"You're right," I said to Nedim. "You don't have to cut them up. You can learn some other way."

Cavit was furious. Realizing that we were quarreling in front of our son, he took me by the arm and led me out of the room. Then he turned on me: "You're not a fit mother. This obsession with animals is ruining the children. If they care that much about animals, they'll be unhappy all their lives. It's better to shut your eyes."

"Nedim must follow his conscience," I insisted.

"Who put that conscience into him in the first place?" he yelled. "You did it! You with all your talk, talk, talk about animals. I've always loved animals, but where I come from we didn't have any of this pamby-namby gluck about 'the poor little animals.' "

185

I hit right back. "Where you come from, I almost died when I saw that little donkey falling down in the street. I saw the way they beat their animals—big, fat men riding on tiny donkeys." I dared one more blow. "And their wives trotting along behind like dogs."

"If you were a Turkish wife, you'd be following me at a respectful distance, instead of giving me any backtalk. And setting yourself above your son's teachers. What kind of a woman are you?"

"I may not be your kind of woman, but I'll fight for my children's right to obey their consciences. You can't take that out of me and I won't let you take it out of the kids."

After we both had calmed down, we spoke more quietly of the brutalizing effect of many aspects of education and social conditioning on the natural sympathies of children. Eventually Cavit agreed that it does greater harm to a child to allow his natural sensitivity to be squelched then to defy authority. Nedim did not dissect the frog.

Since then, Nedim has dissected several animals. But it was done in a good cause and of necessity. For he is now at the University of Michigan, studying to be a veterinary doctor—a fitting choice of vocation for a man who grew up surrounded by animals and a joy to his parents.

To pit oneself against prevailing custom and tradition, no matter in how good a cause, tends to isolate a person. I must admit that at times I felt myself alone and engulfed by insurmountable odds. Especially during hunting season, I sometimes came close to despairing and faltering in my faith that animal life on this earth could be saved through human insight and sympathy. Looking out from the cabin across the lake on inwardly grey days, I felt almost as forlorn as I did at the window in Istanbul so many years ago.

But I always found sustenance in reading the great American naturalists—Muir, Thoreau, Seton, Eiseley, and Krutch—and derived new strength from the works of Dr. Schweitzer, whose every line proclaims a faith distilled in the magic phrase "reverence for life."

Nor did I lack support from like-minded friends, notably Dorothy Cope, that excellent observer of all things in nature, and my photographer friends Merrill Cottrell and Alfred A. Francesconi—both "reformed" hunters—who taught me to widen and sharpen my own vision with the lens of a camera.

It also helped to know that through the Humane Society of the United States my philosophy had organizational backing to the extent that such fragile commodities as love and sympathy can ever be institutionalized. My association with the Humane Society and the Audubon Society led to many rewarding contacts all over the country. As more people heard of Unexpected Wildlife Refuge through these organizations, I enjoyed encouraging visits from many naturalists.

My old mentor, Mr. Duncan, the bluebird man from Kentucky, put me in touch with Mrs. Aida Flemming, the founder of the Kindness Clubs, an international children's organization aimed at encouraging concern for animals among youngsters. Believing that the early years are the crucial time for strengthening and confirming children's natural sympathies, I found my work with the Kindness Clubs particularly challenging and rewarding. To look at the open and eager faces of youngsters as they listen with rapt attention to my animal talks is to me an unfailing source of encouragement and balm for the vicarious wounds I bear whenever the sound of gunfire carries into the refuge.

The area of the refuge had meanwhile been enlarged to nearly two hundred and sixty acres by the purchase of adjacent land, and as more and more people began taking an interest in our work, I began publishing a small newsletter, "Good News from Unexpected," to keep them informed about our animals and about various issues affecting wildlife preservation. "Good News" enjoys a growing circulation, which now stands at about six hundred. Putting out a new issue every month takes a lot of time, but I feel that it is well worth it, for the publication helps to bring the refuge closer to its distant friends. It also helps create a meaningful bond between the refuge and interested people in the surrounding communities.

Another such bond is visits from children in the area. To keep from disturbing the animals, visiting groups must necessarily remain small—usually no more than ten at a time—and of course I cannot guarantee that any animals will come into view while the children are there. But just to be in wild, natural surroundings while hearing firsthand accounts of animal life is a great adventure for children, many of whom have never been outside of urban or suburban areas. By giving such children their first real glimpse of nature, I feel that the refuge has assumed a vital function in addition to providing shelter for animals. It has become an effective working tool for the awakening of human hearts.

There are now signs that such an awakening may be imminent on a larger scale. Certainly it is a good portent that the *New York Times,* the country's most prestigious newspaper, now consistently devotes editorials to the cause of conservation and humane treatment of animals. It is encouraging when such a great newspaper, predominantly devoted to grave national issues, runs the following editorial concerning a fur advertisement in its own pages:

"What glory is there," asks the *Times,* "in wrapping oneself in a lifeless specimen of man's dwindling heritage of nature's wild beauty? What right does man have now to deprive the earth forever of some of its most beautiful and interesting creatures—from polar bear to jaguar to crocodile and turtle—merely to satisfy a passing style whim?"

I feel equally heartened when a mass-circulation magazine like LIFE devotes an entire issue (December 22, 1967) to the subject of wildlife and its preservation. Charles A. Lindbergh contributed a notable essay in which he summarized the theme as follows:

"In wildness, as in no other environment, elements of body, mind, and spirit flux and fuse. . . . The smell of the earth, the touch of leaves, sounds of animals calling, myriad qualities interweave to make one not only aware, but aware of one's awareness."

I have smelled the earth, touched the leaves, and heard the call of animals. And I have been able to respond with all the resources of my mind and of my heart. This has been my good fortune. This has been my unexpected treasure.